THE MODERN DAY LEPER

The Way We See Sex Offenders

Dick Witherow

Copyright 2008 by Dick Witherow

All rights reserved. Written permission must be secured from the publisher to use or reproduce any part of this book, except for brief quotations in critical reviews or articles.

Unless otherwise noted Scripture is taken from the King James Version of the Holy Bible.

Verses marked TLB are taken from *The Living Bible*, copyright © 1971. Used by permission of Tyndale House Publishers, Inc. Wheaton, Illinois 60189. All rights reserved.

Published by: Matthew 25 Ministries, Inc.
P.O. Box 5690
Lake Worth, FL 33466-5690

Editor: Jim Leary

Cover Design: Ron McGurn

ISBN: 1-4392-0829-8
ISBN-13: 9781439208298

Printed By: BookSurge

Printed in the United States of America

DEDICATION

This book is dedicated to my wife Maggie, who is my friend, my helpmate and co-laborer in the ministry for over 25 years. To our totally committed staff; Pat Powers, Nyoka Edwards and Jan TenBarge, without whom this book would not be written. And to the many who have tirelessly served the forgotten men and women behind prison walls. Especially to those who have at great risk to there credibility and reputations endeavored to help those who have been convicted of sexual crimes. And to those who have been the victims of these types of crimes.

FOREWORD

How do we protect our children in a world run amuck? Where do parents turn to obtain information that will relieve the fears that their children will become victims of some form of disaster in a world that appears to be unraveling at the seams? We used to believe that if we provided our children with the kind of education that would make it possible for them to gain a level of affluence, everything would work out fine. (As if success depended on ones status in the professions, or the size of their bank account.) Many have learned that money can't buy happiness. Or, if you haven't discovered the fallacy of that belief system, let me remind you of the many who thought their retirement years were secure, only to find that those who had control over their retirement funds were thieves. Then there is the problem of natural disasters; hurricanes, tornadoes, earthquakes, floods, forest fires, etc. You feel safe and secure, and then, all of a sudden everything you own is gone. Maybe you lost members of your family. Maybe your kids go to college where they are introduced to wild parties where alcohol and drugs flow freely and moral restraints go out the window. Maybe they go off to war in strange lands.

A major concern in today's society is how do we protect our little ones from sexual predators? This book shows that there is a vast difference between sexual predators and sex offenders. It will show that most sex offenders do not deserve the harsh laws that are made to deter sexual predators.

Table of Contents

Chapter 1: Modern Day Lepers 1

Chapter 2: At Risk Kids 5

Chapter 3: A Father's Love 9

Chapter 4: A Myth And Its Effect 19

Chapter 5: A Case Study 25

Chapter 6: Stranger Danger 33

Chapter 7: Monsters 37

Chapter 8: Sex Offenders In Our Communities 43

Chapter 9: Free Indeed 51

Chapter 10: Pain & Addiction 61

Chapter 11: Sex And Recovery Ministry 67

Chapter 12: Justice For All 79

Chapter 13: Prejudice 87

Chapter 14: Fear 91

Chapter 15: By His Love 97

Chapter 16: For Parents 101

Chapter 17: For Pastors 105

Epilogue 111

References 119

We Get Mail 123

Chapter 1
Modern Day Lepers

During the time of Jesus Christ's ministry, Palestinian society faced many of the same social problems that confront us today. As a part of the "worldwide" Roman Empire, the Jewish leaders were as concerned about the welfare of their people in the spiritual, physical, and moral sense as they were in preserving their traditional way of life in a rapidly changing world. Unfortunately, the influences of the Greek, and later the Roman conquerors, often conflicted with the Old Testament Laws of Moses that formed the basis of the day-to-day decision making for devout Jews.

One of the most serious physical and social challenges was controlling the large number of persons with, or suspected of having, Leprosy (now called Hansen's disease). Leprosy was an overwhelmingly terrifying and devastating disease.

The Modern Day Leper

Without the antibiotics invented in the mid-twentieth century, Leprosy was a catastrophic, disfiguring, and ultimately fatal disease. Beginning with simple patches of dry skin, it slowly progressed to the loss of toes, fingers, noses and ears. Larger limbs were eventually lost and the destruction continued until it finally led to death.

Although we now understand that Leprosy is extremely difficult to spread from person to person, at that time the only reasonable means of controlling the disease was by strictly obeying the Old Testament requirements. The sufferers would be isolated for life to avoid any further contacts with healthy people. It's difficult to imagine Christ's willingness to speak with and actually touch the sufferers of the disease. It must have had an impact on both the crowds and the lepers themselves. This example of His devotion to those who were shunned by society is as astonishing today as it was then. The total banishment from any contact with healthy people, and from any charity or kindness was strictly enforced. The lepers were required to live in small, isolated parts of the city or even outside it's protective walls. Many were required to wear a bell, similar to a cow or sheep bell, which alerted other people of their approach. Many cities also required that the leper continually shout, "Unclean, Unclean" as a further warning. The very idea of treating a suffering minority of the population in such a callous manner seems almost insane to us now. The society of first century Israel was also concerned about enforcing Jewish moral standards and religious laws in a secular society. They were deeply influenced by the permissive attitudes of the Greeks, Romans, and Baalists, which included tolerance for homosexuality and even temple prostitution. The Jewish attitude towards even the most non-abusive sexual behaviors of others was at least as negative as those of contemporary politicians. It is the same general attitude today toward anyone labeled a "Sex Offender" no matter what his crime or the circumstances involved.

As illogical and unnecessary as the Leper Laws seem in light of our current understanding of the etiology of Hansen's Disease, contemporary American society continues to call for similar punitive, illogical, counterproductive statutes against released sex offenders. Please understand, we're not trying to justify or forget the damage that sexual assault can do to a child's life. The intent instead, is to show how scientifically valid studies have shown that isolation of sex offenders is unnecessary. It is a waste of human potential, and a waste of public money. These laws deceive people into thinking they will somehow protect their children from predators. A myriad of studies have consistently shown very low rates of re-offense of offenders who have been through the legal system; particularly those who have participated in "Sex Offender Treatment" conducted by a trained counselor or psychologist.

Ironically, some of the same faith groups who preach salvation, redemption, and newness of life are also those who advocate most loudly for extremely long periods of incarceration for all sex offenders, regardless of the seriousness and the number of their offenses. They then argue for a lifetime of stigma of "uncleanness" ensured by

Community Notification Laws. These laws very severely restrict areas of residence, fields of employment, early curfews, and "No Knock" warrant-less searches of the offender's home, car, office, computer, and person.

But, do these expensive, intrusive conditions really prevent additional offenses? Simply put - NO! Carefully controlled research studies have repeatedly shown that the result of these laws make it extremely difficult, if not impossible, for released offenders to re-establish themselves positively in the community. (1) Tragically, there is no evidence that such laws protect children in any way. We will cover this in detail other chapters. We will also show alternative methods to monitor sex offenders in the community.

Chapter 2
At Risk Kids

If you are reading this book and you are a parent or grandparent, I want you to know that your children are at risk. Not only of being sexually molested, but of becoming a sexual offender. Probably 50% of youth between thirteen and eighteen years old will commit a sexual crime before their eighteenth birthday. We are hearing reports of much younger children, some as young as ten, offending. Fortunately most of them will never be arrested. For those that are, there is a good chance they will go to prison and carry the label sex offender for the rest of their lives. They will have to endure all the hardships; housing restrictions, being on the sexual registry, and all the other conditions sexual offenders cope with. In spite of all the publicity about the <u>alleged</u> danger of sexual offenders, this very real danger receives little if any publicity. You will read more about this in future chapters.

The Modern Day Leper

Most sexual crimes are not committed by strangers, but by those in your own family, or by people you know quite well. Your own children or their friends may be guilty of violating a younger sibling or the neighbor's child. It is dangerous for teens to become babysitters if they have not learned how to deal with their sexual urges.

Think back to when you were entering adolescence. Remember the confusion you had when those hormones kicked in? If you had a struggle back then, consider the culture our youth are living in now. Sexual suggestions are thrown at them from every angle. Television programming gives the impression that sexual immorality is to be desired. The lyrics in their music add fuel to the fire. Then there is pornography on the Internet and romance novels. Would you have liked to deal with all that? What little sex education most of our youth get is not only wrong, it encourages them to be sexually active. The public schools tell them; "You will probably have sex, so here take these condoms." What kind of message is that sending?

Have you watched the expose of college kids involved in drinking bouts and sex orgies? I have some bad news for you; many of them were doing those things long before they went to college. It is dangerous for kids growing up in today's society. Peer pressure and the availability of alcohol and drugs make it difficult for many of our youth to avoid these pitfalls.

All is not lost! There is help if you are looking for it. Focus on the Family has some great resources for parents of teens. Check our their website www.family.org. (1) Another great resource is the book **"Love, Sex, and Lasting Relationships"** by Chip Ingram. (2) This book is so powerful it should be mandatory reading by parents and youth alike.

Now, hold onto your hat as we take a realistic look at the sexual exploits of many in today's society. We will pay particular attention to the consequences of those who find themselves accused of a sexual crime.

Chapter 3
A Father's Love

"Perverts! Get that scum out of here! Send them back to prison where they belong!" These are the words of one of our most outspoken critics. When people heard that we operated a program to assist ex-offenders charged with sexual crimes transition back into society, many were outraged. They feared for the safety of their children. But, does it make sense to turn a sex offender loose on the streets without a support group? Does it make sense to deprive a man of the training necessary to live a life free of sexual addictions?

The amount of media attention given to the horrific crimes of rape and murder of innocent children has both a positive and negative effect on the populace. Positive in the fact that it increases awareness of this threat upon our most vulnerable citizens, and negative whereas it instills unwholesome fear in the hearts of parents. You can hardly turn your television on without being bombarded with minute details of the latest assault on one of our children. Does this mean that there is a marked increase in these types of crimes? Actually the numbers are down slightly from what they were a decade ago, but the sensationalizing of these crimes gives the effect that they are on the rise. However, knowing this provides little comfort to those parents that are concerned about the welfare of their children.

How do we protect our children from sexual predators?
This is the heart cry of parents throughout our land today. The general response has been to heed the warnings posted in the newspapers and on the Internet by our law enforcement agencies; especially when one who has been charged with a sexual offense moves into our neighborhood. Will our diligence really protect our children from sexual predators? Is there really any way concerned parents can protect their children from becoming the next victim? There are some things we as parents and grandparents can do, but targeting ex-offenders is not really going to get the job done. While the thought of anyone taking advantage of a child makes our blood boil, is it best to try and rehabilitate the sexual offender or to drive him to despair?

In my 30 years of working with those caught up in addictive lifestyles, I have learned what it takes for men to put their lives back together, and to become a part of the solution rather than a part of the problem. Until recently we had a prison aftercare-training center on a 21-acre ranch, where we conducted a pilot program for sex offenders. We realized the problem we faced when attempting to evaluate the risk involved and the effectiveness of a program of recovery for those charged with sex crimes. Many would say, "These kind never change!" We know differently. We know that when God gets hold of a person's life He changes them from the inside out. Our 12-month, in-residency program has operated successfully. Our center provides a compassionate recovery program for those who were willing to learn how to make viable choices, took responsibility for themselves, and strove to achieve success.

An understanding of the different types of sex crimes and how our society deals with these issues is essential. What we have is a fear of sex offenders that defies reason. Our country is in trouble. Is what we are doing solving the problem of ever increasing sexual perversions? While not forgetting to be cautious of sex offenders, we also need to focus on the origins of the problem. We need to focus on the family.

Does not this problem involve the breakdown of our families? Sixty percent of our nations children are growing up without a father's presence. The result has been an epidemic of alcoholism, drug addiction and sexual perversions among our youth. What is the real threat to our communities? The youth that have been victimized are now victimizing others. Until mothers and fathers learn to communicate love to each other and to their children the problem will just get worse. It is the breakdown of the family that has led to much of the moral decay we see all around us. The recent outbreak of violence in our schools resulting in "kids killing kids" has proven to be a real wake up call that something is drastically wrong. As usual, the politicians have opted for a "quick fix." We have seen a rash of legislative bills designed to strengthen gun laws, increase law enforcement, etc. There has even been a move to allow a little spiritual expression in our public schools, such as a minute of quiet reflection in lieu of prayer to start the school day. **Too little, too late.** Those parents that are deceived into thinking they are loving their children by giving them everything money can buy, have forgotten what they need most. They need parents who love each other and will spend quality time with them. We have already lost a whole generation of our youth. Alcoholism, drug addiction, and sexual promiscuity among our youth has reached epidemic proportions. What will the future hold? Of the thousands of men we have counseled, it is rare to find one who had a healthy relationship with his Dad. **In twenty years of prison ministry, I can't remember even one man whom I counseled, whose father showed him genuine love.** A child growing up without knowing a father's love is damaged merchandise. Through their woundedness may come deviant sexual behavior and addiction.

Men need to learn how to communicate love to their wives and children. That is the only way to stop the breakup of our families, and will do more than anything else in protecting our children

A Father's Love

The biggest threat to our children is not the unlikely chance that a predator will attack them, but that they will not be taught how to deal with their own sexuality. This will set them up for a life devoid of real love and satisfaction. To give you some insight on this issue I quote excerpts taken from an article by a Presidential Candidate, Alan Keyes, titled "Sugarcoating Poison," which was published in the July 2002 issue of the Home Times Newspaper in West Palm Beach, Florida: (1)

"Millions of decent American parents today are forced to wage a continual battle to preserve the innocence of their children, particularly in sexual matters, against a rising tide of morality corrupting influences in the media, government, schools, and in the culture at large. But safeguarding the souls of children largely consists of protecting them from hearing about, or God forbid experiencing perverse possibilities they would never consider on their own. The Planned Parenthood mantra says that the key issue in sexual formation is "education", treating sexuality as if there is a body of factual knowledge that any 13-year-old can acquire that will make him capable of responsible decisions in such matters. Nothing could be more false. <u>The Knowledge that makes humanizing sexual choices possible comes, in part, from moral experience that is simply not available to the young.</u> Sexual responsibility is a crucial part of moral responsibility. That means it requires the formation of character, and of the ability – among other things – to forego present gratification for future goods. Moral responsibility includes the ability to appreciate the importance of things like honor, decency, and obligation to family that may seem abstract in the short term, but turn

out all important to human happiness. It is a simple fact of human experience that the tides of passion begin to swell before the ability to handle those passions can develop. The formation of moral character occurs crucially during the years of maturation and struggle with such passions. The proposal that young children can be beneficially "informed" about and then manage sexual practices is at best utterly morally obtuse. The first and foremost component of sex related education must be family. The first thing that children ought to learn is not physiology, but what it means to be a mother or father and the connection between moral disciplines and the love and tenderness that is shared within a family."

I also take excerpts from an article by Armstrong Williams titled "A Fathers Responsibility," in the same issue of the Home Times.

"The fact is, that from ones parents a child learns what love, anger and affection are. A child learns how to navigate and express his or her emotions. A child can also learn spousal abuse, dishonesty and drug addiction. Men who abandon their duties as a father to pursue drugs or some other vice not only show a lack of their own self worth, but also display to their peers their inability to cope with the duties of life. Many mothers, through no fault of their own, are forced to raise children on their own. Likewise, the mere presence of fathers does not guarantee the best home environment."

Think about your own childhood. What kind of sex education did your parents provide for you? If you are like most of us, your answer will be, "Very little, or none at all." This is not something that can be left to chance. Too often children get their sex education from their peers who are just as ignorant as they are about love and sex. They don't know that their sexuality is a gift from God that enhances our lives when used as our Creator intended. They are unaware that the "evil one" uses our lack of knowledge to destroy lives.

"**When it comes to our God given gift of sexuality, parents must accept their responsibility of educating their children with regards as to how to handle this gift.**" It is normal for children as they come into puberty to become aware of their sexuality and begin to experiment. That is why it is important that parents understand the boundaries God has given for a healthy sex life and impart this knowledge to their children early in life. It is equally important that they role model a healthy sex life to their children. Parents who watch improper television programs or have pornographic magazines around the house are setting their children up for a fall. I'm not just talking about hard-core pornography. Magazines like Playboy or Hustler, or even Sport's Illustrated swim suit edition, falling into a child's hand at the wrong time, can set up a pattern of lust that will lead them into sexual addiction. I believe the greatest threat to our children in today's society is pornography. Ever since the sexual revolution came on the scene in the 50's or 60's, pornography has gained a foothold in our nation. Under the guise of "freedom of speech," greed oriented men have inundated our land with all kinds of filth in print and through the film media. What started out as a trickle has become a flood of perversion and has created an epidemic of sexual addiction among the populace. You don't have to have pornographic magazines in your home. Are your children watching MTV? This is one of the major things that has influenced teenage girls to feed the passions of young men. They are brainwashed into believing they should make themselves sexually attractive in order to be accepted. Television is playing a major role in influencing our youth.

What else are your children watching on the boob tube? The current wave of "Reality" television programs is nothing short of pornographic films. Even watching programming that is rather void of sexual exploitation or innuendo's is not entirely safe. The commercials are using sex to sell their wares.

KNOW THE TRUTH

As you can see, it is best not to be uninformed or misinformed about these matters. Our sexuality is a gift from God. Used properly, it is a wonderful experience, but when used improperly it will cause irreparable harm. Yes, it was God who gave us the gift of sex, but not without boundaries. The Bible says that the marriage bed is undefiled. That means that sex is intended to be used by those who have committed themselves to each other in a marital relationship. Because God intended for the man to be the initiator of sexual encounters He gave him the stronger desire for sex. It should come as no surprise to anyone that most men spend an inordinate amount of time thinking about sex. That is the way they are wired. It is precisely because of this that men are more vulnerable when it comes to being tempted towards sexual perversion. No wonder so many men get entrapped in addiction to pornography. Christian psychologist Steven Arterburn has written a book titled **Every Man's Battle,** (2) which aptly details the struggles men have in keeping their sexuality in check. That is, providing they realize or care that they are in a battle. I cannot emphasize too strongly how important it is that men and women be knowledgeable about these matters. The Bible says, "My people are destroyed by a lack of knowledge." Nowhere is this truer than in the ignorance many have regarding their own sexuality.

Our communities need programs that will assist ex-offenders who demonstrate a strong desire to live productive lives. Lives free of all criminal activities. These programs protect our communities from those who might have been a threat if it were not for the help they received.

Chapter 4
A Myth And Its Effect

Webster's dictionary describes a myth as: An imaginary person or thing; an invented story. It has been said that if you repeat something often enough, people will believe it is factual regardless of the reliability of the statement. Let me tell you about a myth that is affecting a large segment of our society. Somehow the myth got started that 90% of convicted sex offenders commit new sex crimes and are subsequently returned to prison. While popular opinion has it that these people never change, nothing could be further from the truth. The myth that 90% of sex offenders will re-offend is exactly that, **a myth**. According to a fact sheet published by the **National Center on Institutions and Alternative Sentencing**, 87% of once-caught sex offenders do not go on to be re-arrested for a subsequent new sex offense. (1) Hardly a day goes by that we don't see a report on the evening news about someone being arrested for a sex crime. Generally our impression is, "another sex offender being re-arrested." However, if you listen closely, you will usually find this is not a convicted sex offender, but a new offender. While the nay Sayers in the news media and some legislators continue to propagate the myth of high recidivism for convicted sex offenders, their reporting is not based on corroborative data. **NCIA's** information shows that their recidivism figures have been substantiated by multiple studies. The problem is that our legislators, on the basis of the aforementioned myth, are establishing laws that make it extremely difficult for once convicted sex offenders who complete their prison terms to be able to find housing and employment. To add to the dilemma, local administrators of the zoning codes and the general public have been so influenced by these myths that ministries that have the capability of assisting these people are not able to function.

The problems these men face in attempting to find employment and housing once they are released are enormous. Immediately upon release from prison a sex offender must register at the driver's license office. This is so they can be listed in a national database. Every time they move they must re-register within 24 hours. They must also report to the local Sheriff's office and their probation office. The Sheriff's office puts a notice in the local newspaper as to where they will be living, and often announces this information on a local TV station. This information is also put on an Internet database that can be accessed by anyone who has a computer. Sheriff Deputies sometimes canvass the area where this individual will be living and warn the neighbors that this "dangerous" sex-offender is moving into their neighborhood. If their crime involved a minor child, they are not permitted to live within 1,000 feet of any place where children congregate. This includes schools, parks, churches, and daycare centers. Can you imagine how difficult it is for them to find a residence that doesn't have any of these places within 1,000 feet? The latest law passed by our Florida legislators says they cannot live within 1,000 feet of a school bus stop. This has tightened the noose on former sex offenders that were living productive lives in our communities. **Come, let us reason together**. Does anyone think for one minute that placing a 1,000-foot invisible barrier from where there might be unattended children is going to deter anyone bent on harming our children? A sexual predator is not likely to commit crimes that close to where he lives! Recently in Okeechobee, Florida we became involved in three incidences where former sex offenders that had secured housing were ordered to move within 24 hours or be arrested because it was found that they were in violation of this new law. In one incident Sheriff Deputies were ready to put handcuffs on the man before we were able to intervene. These men would have gone to jail if we had not been able to help them.

Think for a moment at the notification done by law enforcement. If you were a landlord would you risk the wrath of your neighbors by renting to one who is so branded? I have grandchildren, and if there is a dangerous sexual predator in the area, I certainly want to know it. But <u>only</u>

The Modern Day Leper

<u>one percent of those convicted of sex crimes are dangerous predators</u>. While these laws are not really doing anything to protect our children, they make it extremely difficult for those sex offenders who are not a risk to our children, to find housing.

I have listed only a few of the problems confronting former sex offenders. There are others that also make it extremely difficult for them to make a successful transition back into our communities. I submit that these strong arm methods are not helping to keep these men from re-offending, but rather are driving many into despair, making them more likely to re-offend. Rather than making it easier to monitor their activities, we are forcing many of these men to abandon their attempts to conform to these oppressive conditions and go underground. When that happens, we have defeated the purpose for which these laws were passed. We have lost the ability to monitor their activities.

A few years ago we would hear accounts of how communist governments had become police states that monitored every movement of their citizens. We were appalled. Is what we are doing to this segment of our society any less oppressive?

Continually harassing those who have served their time is not going to protect our children from sex offenders. We covered how to protect your children from sex offenders in chapter three.

A Myth And Its Effect

Fifty years ago a handful of people started a sexual revolution. They declared we should break off the bonds of sexual restraint and America started down a slippery slope. Their cry was for "sexual freedom." Sex never was free, and today we are paying the price for opening the door that has led to so much depravity. We need to get back to the moral values that this nation had 50 years ago, when sex wasn't being promoted in the media and marriage and family were honored. We need a new sexual revolution. We need to make a radical 180-degree change and get back to sexual purity.

In the year 2000, Matthew 25 Ministries established an aftercare program to assist ex-offenders who had been charged with committing sexual crimes. They were very successful in operating that program until a zoning problem forced them to close in 2003. Given only 10 days to close their facility, neither their clients nor their staff was able to find housing in any county that was acceptable by the Probation Department for the 14 men they had to relocate. It was very difficult to find either a program or a housing situation that probation officers would approve. <u>This is a national problem</u>. We need to be addressing this problem.

We're not just talking about statistics, but people's lives. In our sex saturated society it is not uncommon for someone to become involved in activities that would lead him or her to cross over the line and commit a sex crime. Often this offender is so devastated once their crime is discovered that they cry out to God for help. We serve a God that hears these types of cries and He is a God of grace and mercy for all men. Yes, even for convicted sex offenders. I have been involved in prison ministry since 1972 and have worked with hundreds of these men. I know the sincerity of so many in wanting to live lives that are pleasing to God. Unfortunately, when this person completes his sentence and attempts to find a support group that will help him overcome the hurdles he must face, usually he finds all doors have been closed.

Given all the public has been bombarded with, is it any wonder that their minds are made up; that they believe the horror stories? But, the public has been hoodwinked! They continue to believe that all sex offenders continue to re-offend in part because they have never seen any of the studies regarding the numbers that do not re-offend. They have not been made aware of the actual statistics, which have been documented by the National Center on Institutions and Alternative Sentencing, and the United States Department of Justice. They show that a larger majority of convicted sex offenders do not commit new sex offences. (1) (2)

Chapter 5
A Case Study

Dick was raised in a home with an alcoholic father and an abusive mother; his childhood was not a happy one. He received no formal sex education. Rather his playmates introduced him to pornographic material at age ten. It was then that he learned what it meant to be sexually aroused and how to give himself pleasure through masturbation. Being shy and withdrawn, he spent many hours in these activities. When he was twelve, he performed oral sex on his little sister who was only four. He felt such shame, that he never violated her again. His father had died two years earlier and the abuse at the hands of his mother became greater. When he was seventeen he left home, joined the Army, and was sent to Germany. At this point his drinking, which had started a year earlier, became a problem. Alcohol helped him overcome his feelings of inferiority and made him feel like a man. Upon his discharge from the Army, after serving only 22 months, he met and fell in love with a 15-year old girl. Early in their relationship they became sexually active. She became pregnant, and they wanted to get married. However, when the authorities were made aware of the situation, he was charged with sexual battery with a child under 16 and given a five-year prison sentence. He served his sentence and was released with 10 years probation, along with the label "Sex Offender."

Early in his incarceration Dick attended a chapel service, and heard that Jesus had paid the penalty for his sins. He recognized his need to get right with God and asked Jesus to save him. He became a regular at the chapel services and began attending a support group that helped inmates overcome addictions to alcohol and drugs. He was able to stop drinking (although alcohol and drugs are contraband, they are found in prison), and was also able to quit smoking.

While he was in prison, television newscasters determined that the sensationalism of sex crimes increased their ratings. Politicians jumped on the public's interest, and passed laws that placed heavy restrictions on sex offenders.

Upon his release he was given $100 dollars and told he must report to his probation officer and have a place of residence within 48 hours. His plan was to move back in with his mother, but because she lived close to a playground, it was not allowed, (sex offenders are not permitted to live

A Case Study

within 1,000 feet of any place where children congregate). He had friends looking for housing for several months prior to his release, but none could be found. The only place they found that didn't get eliminated due to the 1,000-foot rule wouldn't rent to him because of the notoriety the landlord would be subject to for renting to this sex offender. His place of residence would be recorded on the sexual offender registry on the Internet, along with a notice placed in the local newspaper. Sometimes the sheriff's department will hand out flyers (with the offenders photograph) to the neighbors. In addition to these restrictions, he was required to report each month to his probation officer. Also he was required to attend weekly sex therapy classes, with polygraph testing. He is made to wear an ankle bracelet and carry a satellite-monitoring box that carries a $30 monthly fee. The cost of his probation supervision is another $30 a month. The sex therapy classes add another $120 to $159 per month charge, and the polygraph testing ran $300 the first year. These heavy financial costs are mandatory for many released sex offenders.

His first day of freedom is taken up with his need to register at the driver's license office, and the sheriff department, then with his probation officer. Since each of these places are in different parts of town, he is fortunate that a friend agreed to take a day off work and transport him to the various agencies. His probation officer informed him that he would not be permitted to leave the county without permission, and then only for the sake of employment. He would not be permitted to leave the state for any reason, even for a death in the family. Since he has not been able to find a place to live that qualifies under the 1,000-foot rule, the probation officer tells him of a motel where he can spend the night. He pays $56 for the motel room and finds he now has $22 of his $100 left. He told his friend goodbye and went to a nearby restaurant to get a bite to eat. Returning to his motel room, the enormity of his problems hits him like a ton of bricks. He is broke, without a job, and no place to live. He only has another 24 hours to find a permanent place to live or have his probation violated and return to prison. Although never having been involved in criminal activities, he begins to have thoughts of how he can steal some money and a car and hit the road. He knows he will need to get out of the state, maybe even out of the country. He will need to establish a new identity and live as a fugitive from justice. What other choice does he have?

Saved in the nick of time! His friend calls him at the motel to let him know of a ministry that helps ex-offenders overcome the obstacles they face upon their release from prison. There are very few programs that help sex offenders. This causes us to ask: "What is going to happen to thousands of former prisoners that do not have this kind of support group to assist them"? It is very difficult for many ex-offenders, (those who have not been charged with a sexual offence) to start over again. For those who have served time for having committed a sexual crime (even consensual sex) it is becoming intolerable. Are they permitted to lead a normal life upon their release? Not hardly! These days, all convicted sex-offenders must serve years of probation following their prison sentence. They are in danger of having their probation violated for any number of reasons. We know of incidences where men have been violated for being asleep and consequently didn't answer the door when their probation officer came to the house to check on them. We know of one who had to spend two months in jail before he was cleared on that very technical violation. Our legislators are continually passing new legislation that further tightens the noose on sex-offenders. Unfortunately, they haven't done their homework to see if these laws will make our communities safer. A major problem is that for the most part, there is no real plan in effect to properly classify the degree of risk of each offender. When you throw all sex-offenders into the same fish bowl, you make it difficult for law enforcement to monitor those who pose the greatest threat. Are we treating them like animals by putting monitors on them?

According to the recently passed Jessica Lunsford Act in Florida, any adult committing a sex crime against a child 12 years of age or younger will receive a life sentence, 25 years mandatory. A convicted sex offender who commits any type of sex crime will also receive a life sentence, 25 years mandatory. If we could be sure that everyone accused of these crimes is guilty, and is the pervert they are made out to be, these stiff sentences might have some merit. All too often this is not the case. Those charged with sexual crimes are already receiving longer sentences than those charged with other types of crime.

The Modern Day Leper

The hysteria that has caused our legislatures to pass this and other recent laws dealing with sex offenders has a downside. Consider again the conditions now facing those who have completed their prison terms and are released on probation (all sex offenders have years of probation tacked onto their sentences). Restricting them from living within 1,000 feet of anyplace where children congregate, including school bus stops has caused a revolving door situation. Because they cannot find housing within 48 hours that will conform to these restrictions many have their probation violated and are on their way back to prison. This, in spite of the fact that there is no evidence that shows that restricting where a sex offender may live has proved to be a deterrent to one bent on attacking children. Couple this with those studies that show that 87% of sex offenders <u>do not</u> go on to commit new sex crimes and you can see how we are doing a grave injustice to those who have paid for their crimes and want the opportunity to live as law abiding citizens.

How is this going to affect our prison population? How many times have you heard those running for public office make this statement; "If elected I vow to protect you the people, for I'm going to get tough on crime"? This has always been a proven vote getter. Has our "getting tough on crime" made our streets safer? You be the judge! Not only are our streets not safe, we have created a prison system that keeps growing and growing. This has created a tax burden that threatens to engulf us. It took our nation 200 years to incarcerate 1,000,000 of its citizens, but only 20 years to reach the second million in 1995! Since that time we have continued to swell our prison population each year. In recent years our legislatures have passed laws that will greatly increase our prison population. It used to be that a convicted felon could get out early for good behavior. Now he must complete 85% of his sentence before becoming eligible for probation. New sentencing guidelines are causing judges to give stiffer and stiffer sentences for many crimes. Nowhere is this truer than for those who are convicted of sexual crimes. Consider that many are now given life sentences. Will this swell our prison population even more rapidly? Absolutely! When they pass these laws I don't think they project the cost to our taxpayers. **Direct and indirect cost of crime in America is now costing taxpayers a staggering $193 billion per year!** Would you like to see that figure double in 20 years? When will we find a way to stop this runaway freight train?

With our policy of getting tough on crime by giving longer sentences we have not only swelled the ranks of those that are in prison, we have also developed a ticking time bomb. More and more un-rehabilitated prisoners are completing their sentences and will soon be released. With longer prison sentences we have seen a reduction in crime statistics, but what is going to happen when this flood of prisoners who have completed their sentences are released?

We believe prison ministry has some solid answers. Not just ministry to prisoners, but to their families as well. Ministry to correction officers and their families, and ministry to the

The Modern Day Leper

victims of crimes. Last but not least, a ministry to released prisoners that helps them maneuver that rough road of integrating back into a society where they have yet to learn how to live as law-abiding citizens.

Chapter 6
Stranger Danger

A sex offender moves into your neighborhood. What should be your response? Well, if you are like most people, your initial reaction will probably be fear. Fear for the safety of your children. But, is that fear based on reality or is it only a perceived threat? With all the publicity surrounding the horrendous crimes against children the public gets the impression that these crimes are commonplace and that "sex offenders" are committing them. The truth is that cases where children are kidnapped and sexually assaulted are extremely rare. Even more rare are instances where convicted sex offenders commit these crimes. According to a report by the U.S. Department of Justice of approximately 4,300 child molesters who were released from prisons in 15 States in 1994, only 3.3% were rearrested for another sex crime. (1) **We should also know that less than 3%**

of convicted sex offenders are pedophiles that stalk children.

If those in the business of reporting news would get the true facts we wouldn't be seeing so much fear and hysteria concerning sex offenders.

How would you feel if your son at 18 had consensual sex with his girlfriend who was only 16 and found himself a convicted sex offender? He may go to prison and most certainly will be on probation for five or more years and have to conform to the residential restrictions of a sex offender. He now goes on the national registry for <u>life</u>. Twenty years pass and the national registry shows him as being 38 years of age and having sex with a sixteen year old. Those who see his picture on the national registry and don't know that he was only 18 at the time of the offense, picture him as the worst kind of pervert.

Is there really any danger of our children becoming a victim of a sexual assault? Absolutely! We are told that one in five girls and one in seven boys will be sexually abused before they are eighteen. **Most of these assaults aren't committed by strangers, but by those the child knew.** (2)

As parents we should be very careful of relatives, friends, teachers, coaches, etc. that are spending an inordinate amount of time and showing a lot of kindness to our children. There are many more instances of fondling than there are of rape but this kind of molestation can cause serious problems later in life.

Many who were themselves sexually abused, have an inordinate fear of anyone who is classified as a sex offender. That is understandable, but it doesn't excuse them of the need to realize that not all who carry that label are a threat to their children.

The next time you see a reported sex crime on the evening news, don't assume a sex offender did it. Rarely is this true. **Most sex crimes reported on the news are <u>new offenders</u>**. The following needs to be reported: "Sexual addiction is no respecter of persons. People from all walks of life are caught up in immoral and often illegal activities. Teachers, police and correctional officers, prosecuting attorneys, even judges have been arrested and charged with sex crimes". These are the ones who are supposed to protect our children and us.

Is it any wonder so many are becoming addicted to sex? We are now living in a sex-saturated society. Check the content of the programs that are being shown on prime time television. How does it compare to what we watched twenty years ago? At 12 billion dollars a year, the revenues of the pornography industry in the U.S. are bigger than the revenues received by ABC, NBC, and CBS combined! On the web there are an estimated 4.2 million porn sites hosting 372 million pages of X rated content. Today, the average age when a boy is first exposed to pornography is <u>eleven</u>. **The real danger to our children is not that they will be sexually assaulted by a stranger, but that they will be violated by someone they trust who has become addicted to porn.** Of no less danger is that our children will themselves become addicted to porn and become the violator. **A statistic from the U.S. Department of Justice shows that 40% of victimized children under age 6 were violated by those under the age of eighteen.**

Studies show that 88% of child molestations are never reported. Then how do the laws targeting convicted offenders protect our communities? Since studies have also shown that convicted sex offenders are the least likely to re-offend, what about the neighbor who is a closet sex addict? How then are we protecting our children by focusing on convicted sex offenders?

Chapter 7
Monsters

We should be concerned with the present hysteria surrounding the fear of sex-offenders. The courts and our legislators have put us on a course that makes our judicial system a travesty of justice. Case in point: Joe had no history of sexual deviancy and is charged with Sexual Battery/Coercing a Child, Sexual Battery/Threatening with a Deadly Weapon, and Lewd & Lascivious Actions on a Child under 16. Charges he vehemently denies. The charges stemmed from one alleged incident involving a child of the woman he was living with and engaged to marry. The accused states that these charges were the result of his breaking off the relationship he had with the alleged victim's mother. He is arrested and spends two years in jail awaiting trial. He cannot afford an attorney and a public defender is assigned his case. In our country an accused is supposed to be presumed innocent until proven guilty. You can throw that out if you are accused of a sexually related crime. Especially if the alleged victim is a child. If you cannot afford to hire an attorney the court will assign a public defender as your defense council. In these situations usually your own attorney will treat you as one who is guilty of all charges. In this particular case, during the two years our subject was in jail, he rarely saw his public defender. When he did, the attorney would only tell him he needed to accept the plea bargain offered by the prosecuting attorney or face spending the next 25 years of his life in prison. He was told that the prosecutor holds all the cards and that he doesn't have a prayer if he insists on going to trial. With two years of this type of psychological pressure he succumbs and accepts a plea bargain of 8 years probation. The fact that the state's attorney was willing to give him probation without any prison time tells us the case against him was very weak. Not being familiar with these matters, Joe had no clue. Nor did he understand that by accepting a plea bargain, he forfeited all rights of appeal. Neither was he made aware of the difficulties he would face in attempting to meet the conditions of his probation.

Things begin to look up for him. He is accepted into a Christian Prison Aftercare program. He tells the director that while in jail, he was led to the Lord by a fellow inmate. He does well and graduates this 12-month program. Later he meets a lady and after a short courtship, they become husband and wife. They run into difficulties in finding a place to live for two reasons. First because no one wants to rent to someone whom the neighbors will be told is a sex-offender, and secondly because he is listed as a "Predator" and is not permitted to live within 1,000 feet of any place where children congregate. That includes schools, parks, playgrounds, daycare centers, etc. He also has difficulty finding meaningful employment due to his record, and has to settle for a job far below his capabilities. Finances become a problem because in addition to paying for his probation supervision, he is required to attend weekly sexual therapy sessions, which include polygraph tests. But he is making it. That is, until in church one day, a young lady asks how he likes the flower she has in her hair. He says, "It looks nice, if you water it, you might have a nice garden." Later that day this 14 year old tells her mother that our subject approached her and said, "I like the flower in your hair, I'd like to water it and make a garden." She then tells her mother, she didn't like the way he looked at her. Now our subject has been attending this church for 6-months and has been active with the praise and worship team, without any incidents. But the mother, knowing that he is classified as a sexual predator is naturally concerned. She calls the sheriff's office asking what restrictions he has with regards being around minors. She is told that he is not permitted to be around unsupervised minors. The sheriff's office reported the matter to the probation office, which has a **zero tolerance** policy in place with regards sexual predators. Our subject is arrested and placed in jail on a charge of violating his probation. His regular probation officer was not in the office that day, and it was the supervisor who ordered the subject arrested without any investigation into the incident.

The Modern Day Leper

As the director of the prison aftercare program that our subject was in, I know that he would not do anything to harm this young lady, or violate her in the way he is accused. I know him well, and I know of the love he has for the Lord and for his fellow man.

In spite of the fact that the accused was attending church with numerous people present when he had this brief discourse with the young lady, the presiding judge found him guilty of violating the conditions of his probation that says he is not allowed unsupervised contact with minors. The judge sentenced him to 20 years in prison. I was shocked to learn that a person on probation who is found guilty of violating one of the terms of his probation can be sentenced based on all his past charges, even though he has never had the opportunity to refute those charges in a court of law. This is one of many fallacies when one accepts a plea bargain rather than taking his case to trial. More about this is covered in chapter ten, **Justice For All**.

Again, the sad part is that if on the original charge our subject would have had a defense council that would have considered his claim of innocence and truly tried to defend him, I doubt if he would have been found guilty on those charges. Consequently, all of what followed would have been avoided.

This is just one case. These kinds of things are happening in our courts every day. No one is safe. You could be wrongly accused of a sexual crime and be subject to these injustices.

Monsters

It isn't just the innocent. How about the person who was guilty of a sexual offense and served his time in prison? Is he or she permitted to lead a normal life upon his or her release? (Yes, women are also charged with sex crimes) Not hardly! In the times in which we are living, all convicted sex-offenders must serve years of probation following their prison sentence. They are constantly in danger of having their probation violated for any number of reasons. I submit that the strong-arm methods used today are not helping to keep these men and women from re-offending. Rather, they are driving many into despair. This in turn makes them more likely to re-offend.

Our hearts go out to the families of the victims of rape and murder. The reaction to these horrendous crimes by the media and our legislators has caused additional laws to be passed in an effort to protect our children. Will these laws accomplish the task for which they are intended? I think not. <u>If they only targeted the one to two percent of sex offenders whose criminal history shows a tendency of violent behavior, or stalking children, they might be beneficial</u>. But, when these laws target all those charged with a sexual offense they are only going to add to the problem. The laws that were already on the books have not changed the danger one iota; in fact they have compounded the problem.

Our legislators have passed laws mandating longer prison sentences and longer probation periods upon completion of those sentences. These mandated prison sentences tie the hands of judges who might take into consideration

The Modern Day Leper

extenuating circumstances when imposing a sentence. As such, our society will need to build more prisons to handle the increase in prison population caused by these longer sentences. We the taxpayers will have to foot the bill for building and operating these new prisons.

Finally, all sex-offenders are not monsters. Yes, some have made horrendous mistakes. Society is creating a monster by believing the lie that: "these type never change." Unless we can find a way to enlighten our society, this monster will turn around and bite us.

Chapter 8
Sex Offenders In Our Communities

Restricting where convicted sex offenders can live.

Many of those who have served their prison sentence for sexual crimes and are eligible to be released on probation cannot find housing that will conform to the restrictions of not living within 1,000 feet of where children congregate. This has become even more difficult with local communities passing ordinances increasing the "safe zone" to 1,500 or 2,500 feet. Since the conditions of probation stipulate that the probationer must provide his probation officer with a valid address within 48 hours of their release, many are not able to comply and have their probation violated. That means they are headed back to prison. Not because they did anything wrong, they just couldn't find any place to live that would meet the safe zone restrictions. In some cases

The Modern Day Leper

Department Of Corrections Classification Officers refuse to release them if they are not able to supply an approved address. In other cases some are taken directly from prison to a county jail to await a hearing for violating this condition of their probation.

Nicki Delson, a licensed clinical social worker who has worked for 30 years with sex offenders and their victims and who is chairwoman of the California Coalition on Sexual Offending says: "Under the guise of "protecting our communities," without a shred of empirical support and in spite of significant empirical evidence to the contrary, sex offenders who served their sentences are being forced to leave their homes (and sometimes families) because they live too close to a school, playground or park ". (1) Jill Levinson, a professor at Lynn University in Boca Raton, Florida says: "Restricting where parolees live can actually do more harm than good. Such requirements tend to push them out of metropolitan areas where they are further away from job opportunities, families, treatment options and all the things we know that will reduce recidivism".* (2)

* Recidivism: The tendency of an offender to repeat criminal acts and patterns of antisocial behavior.

There is more to the sufferings of those who have been convicted of sex crimes. Not only do they find it difficult to survive with all the restrictions and conditions of probation, their families suffer also.

Imagine what it would be like for a wife to lose her husband, and the children to lose their father, during those years when the sex offender is in prison. But, comes the day of his release. There is cause for rejoicing! Not necessarily. If his crime involved a minor child, he is not permitted to live within 1,000 feet of anyplace where children congregate. This invisible buffer zone is even larger in many locales, sometimes as much as 2,500 feet. This causes many families to have to try and find a place to live that will conform to these rigid conditions. If there are minor children in the home, the former offender is not permitted to live there.

We are not talking about families with unlimited resources. Usually these are those who struggle with being on the lower rung of the economy. Consider that during the years of her husband's incarceration, she had become the only breadwinner.

Put yourself in the wife's shoes for just a moment. She is overjoyed. After years of absence, her man is coming home! Now, her joy is turned to mourning. **How are they going to cope with these conditions of his probation?**

The children have their problems too. If their daddy is not permitted contact with them, how do they comprehend this? Compounding this problem is the abuse they receive from their peers as a result of their father being on the national sex offender registry. Kids can be so cruel. We are often told of instances where these children have lost their close friends and have been taunted when their playmates call their father a pervert.

Another problem with the national registry is that of vigilantism. Some sex offenders have been murdered because vigilantes have learned where they lived from the registry. Some families have been harassed with threats and hate mail.

In working with the ex-offender, we see their agony in wanting to be with their loved ones and being denied this basic need. When this burden is added to the other oppressive conditions of their probation it can be overwhelming.

We need to come to the realization that when a sex offender is sentenced, his family is sentenced also. When you undermine the stability of the family, you are laying a foundation for future problems. It is well known that when the father is absent his children are more likely to fall into destructive habits. This is part of the generational curse.

What is the solution? It is imperative that their be a classification of risk and those who do not now present a high risk to re-offend be permitted to live with their families without the housing restrictions. And that where possible their name be removed from the national and local registries. The way the law is today, all sex offenders are treated the same, and the laws governing them are all based on those who have committed the most horrific crimes and/or have had multiple victims. Most sex offenders do not fall under

Sex Offenders In Our Communities

those guidelines and are minimum risk to re-offend. Should we continue to punish them and their families?

Sample Case: Bernard G. has served 10 years of a 15-year sentence for having consensual sex with his under-aged girlfriend. He is due to be released with 10 years probation. If he is not able to find approved housing he will have his probation violated and he will need to serve the remaining 5 years of his original sentence and then be released to serve his 10 years probation. What if he still cannot meet the housing restrictions; will he serve the 10-year probation period in prison? Multiply this case a thousand times and look at the cost of housing these men in prison, when they could have been living productive lives in our communities. In Florida it cost **$21,000** per year to house an inmate.

It should be noted that only 1 to 3% of those charged with sexual crimes are a true predator that are a risk to society. The vast majority of those charged with sexual crimes have never stalked a child, and are not a threat to ever commit another sexual offence. Are we willing to pay the price tag of keeping low risk offenders in prison? Most of them will be released someday. Will they be those who believe in our system of justice, or will they be embittered and more prone to violence?

(b) The national registry.

The public has not been educated regarding the degree of risk of those charged with sexual crimes. Therefore, those who are not predators and are not a threat to our communities are forced to comply with the same restrictions as those who are high risk. Those restrictions include: where they can live, work, and travel. They must pay for probation supervision and for mandated sex therapy sessions. Most will remain on the local and national registry for the rest of their natural lives. By applying the same rules to all sex offenders without regard to degree of risk, we make it more difficult to monitor those who are the greatest risk.

POSSIBLE REMEDIES:

(a) Revisit laws affecting sex offenders.

The public, including our legislatures, must be made aware of the fact that they have been duped into a false belief system that says; "**These kind never change.**" The news media in their quest for sensationalism have perpetrated this lie so much, that it has become accepted as being true. This has caused our legislatures to pass laws that have taken away the constitutional rights of those who have been charged with sex crimes, regardless of the degree of risk to the general public.

In July 2006 Florida Congressman Mark Foley stated on the Fox News Network, "These kind never change. We have the facts. 100% of sex offenders will commit new sex crimes. We just don't know when." I wonder where he got his facts? At the time, then Congressman Foley, was being interviewed along with "America's Most Wanted" John Walsh. They were in Washington D.C. lobbying for the bill that was eventually passed establishing a national Internet database for convicted child molesters.

If, "These kind never change," is a lie, what is truth? All it takes is a little research. The U.S Department of Justice reports a study of sex offenders from 15 states that were released from prison in 1994. Tracking these 9,691 sex-offenders for three years, the results showed that only **5.3%** were rearrested for another sex crime. Not 100% as stated by Congressman Foley. The 9,691 released sex offenders included 4,295 men who were in prison for child molestation. (3)

Our legislatures need to revisit these laws that have been passed with an eye to making some revisions, if and when they see the problems they have caused. There really needs to be a classification of the degree of risk, rather than throwing all offenders into the same fish bowl.

(b) Don't hinder those who are trying to assist sex offenders successfully reenter society.

Our experience has been that local planning and zoning departments have used zoning laws as a way of keeping organizations from establishing locations where they can conduct their programs. Sad to say, but police agencies and county commissioners have been in the forefront of resisting the efforts of having these programs in their communities.

The Modern Day Leper

It needs to be recognized that these organizations are an asset to the community, not a liability. The problem of how we deal with sex offenders coming into our communities needs to be addressed in an intelligent manner, not based on hysteria. We know that we cannot continue to keep these people in prison indefinitely. Some day they are going to get out. What is the best way of helping them become productive citizens again?

In the example we gave earlier regarding Bernard G.; this man had an encounter with the Living God while in prison and turned his life over to Christ. During the five plus years I have known him, I can testify that he truly is a changed person and is no longer a threat to society.

Chapter 9
Free Indeed

This problem of sexual lust has plagued man ever since the beginning of time. One subject you will hardly ever hear preached in church is that concerning our sexuality. Why? Because church folk don't have problems in this area? Hardly! There are probably as many in the church that are caught up in lust as those outside. Unlike many obvious sins, this sin often goes undetected. There is a book titled "The Secret Sin" which tells how sexual sins are commonplace among Church going people. Those who are caught up in these sins are good at keeping their secrets. But, there is One from whom we cannot hide our sins. The Word declares, *"You already know how to please God in your daily living, for you know the commands we gave you from the Lord Jesus himself. Now we beg you-yes, we demand of you in the name of the Lord Jesus-that you live more and more closely to that ideal. For God wants you to be holy and pure, and to keep clear of all sexual sin so that each of you will marry in holiness and honor-not in lustful passion as the heathen do, in their ignorance of God and His ways"* (1Thessalonians 4:1-5LB).

Now we may have a problem in all this, if we do lust, and if we allow ourselves to fall into all manner of sexual sin. For a long time I rationalized my sin by thinking, "God understands why I do the things I do, He made me this way"! Is that true? Well, in a way yes. God did give us our sexual drive. He is the one who invented sex, not Playboy Magazine publisher Hugh Hefner. But, we are the ones who perverted that which God made holy. God didn't cause me to sin. I chose to. When I did, sin got hold of me, and I became increasingly more sinful, more perverted until I was a slave to my sins. God gave us our sexual drive and He knew what He was doing when He did it. We were created as sexual beings, but not without boundaries. Men and women are physically attracted to one another. Many relationships are started based on that physical attraction, but for a relationship to be healthy it must move beyond that initial attractiveness. You also need to know that God established marriage as the only place where the sexual act can be performed within the will of God. God ordained sexual intercourse as a means of fulfilling the bonds of love between a husband and wife, to reproduce, and as a reward for their being faithful to submit to one another in love. Do you know that it is not easy to be submissive and loving

Free Indeed

towards one another in this close intimate relationship called marriage? Hebrews 13:4 says, **Marriage is honorable in all, and the bed undefiled: but whoremongers and adulterers God will judge.** God is letting us know He has ordained sex for those who are married, and He will judge those who violate His commandments and live immorally. How serious is this? 1 Corinthians 6:9, 10 LB says, **"Don't you know that those doing such things have no share in the kingdom of God? Don't fool yourselves. Those who live immoral lives, who are idol worshippers, adulterers or homosexuals-will have no share in His kingdom. Neither will thieves or greedy people, drunkards, slanderers, or robbers".**

SEX EDUCATION

Sex education is not something that should be left to our educators who don't know the Author of our sexuality. Godly parents should teach their children how to deal with their sexuality. I never received any sex education in school, or from my parents. I learned all I knew about sex from my friends who knew nothing about the origin and purpose of sex. Furthermore, not knowing anything about God and His ways, I grew up with a distorted idea of how to deal with my sexuality. Consequently, I developed a fascination for pornographic material, and a masturbation habit that became a stronghold in my life. To be sure, fornication and adultery were by-products of those strongholds. I thought that when I got married I would be free of these bondages. I found out that getting married did not set me free from sexual sin. How many reading this are married and still have a problem with lust? It takes the power of God to break free of those chains!

DELIVERANCE

Is it possible to be set free from life controlling addictions that keep us in bondage? Addictions to such things as cigarettes, alcohol, drugs, and sexual lust? The answer is an unequivocal, **YES!** However, there are several things we must be aware of first.

The main thing we must know is that while we are powerless over our sin, God is ready, willing, and able to give us His power to conquer our addiction. However, we cannot receive God's help unless we are in a right relationship with Him. The only way we can be in a right relationship with God is to receive forgiveness for all the sins we have committed and will commit. This is accomplished from start to finish by believing on the One whom God chose to be a sacrifice for our sins. Jesus Christ took the punishment we deserve for sins when He was nailed to a cross almost 2,000 years ago. Three days after He was buried, He rose from the grave proving that He had conquered sin and death, <u>and that His claims to be God were true.</u> That same resurrection power is available to us today, when we believe. I was 40 years old (seven years after I was saved), when I was baptized in the Holy Spirit. It was then that Jesus set me free of my addictions to alcohol, drugs, cigarettes, lust, and gambling. I found out that God's power is shown forth in our weaknesses, and that, *"He who the Son sets free, is free indeed"* (John 8:36)

Yes, God will do His part to set His people free, but we have an important role to play. We need to trust God, and let Him take away our fears. God is love, and His perfect love casts out all fears. <u>We have been afraid that we cannot conquer our addictions</u>. While this is true in the natural, we need to know that when we are in Christ Jesus, we have dwelling within us the power of a supernatural God. We need to know that to try and overcome addictions in our own strength is an effort in futility. Flesh warring against flesh will lose every time. The Apostle Paul understood that in and of himself he could not rise above his weaknesses. God told Paul, *"My power shows up best in weak people"* (2 Corinthians 12:9 LB). The Word of God further declares, *"I can do everything God asks me to with the help of Christ who gives me the <u>strength and power</u>"* (Philippians 4:13 LB). You see, God never asks us to do anything that He doesn't equip us to do. How cruel would it be for God to tell us, *"Be holy as I am Holy,"* and then not equip us to do that?

There is probably no other area of our lives where we are more vulnerable than our sexuality. Especially men. We have been given strong desires in this area. There are two areas which when kept in proper perspective are healthy, but when out of balance are extremely unhealthy. They are our desire for food and our desire for sexual fulfillment. The one we can't live without and the other many think they can't live without. We need to know what we are dealing with and how God provides. Those who are not married need to recognize how vulnerable they are. Most singles desire a mate, and deal regularly with loneliness. God knows that, for it was He who declared, **"It is not good that the man should be alone"** (Genesis 2:18). The Bible also says, **"The man who finds a wife finds a good thing; she is a blessing to him from the Lord"** (Proverbs 18:22 LB). But you want to be sure that the one you get for a mate is the one God selects. A Godly mate is truly a blessing from the Lord.

BEING SINGLE

The single person needs to know God has a gift for you. It is called celibacy! You can't get this gift anywhere else except from your Heavenly Father. This gift of celibacy wasn't designed just for Catholic Priests and Nuns. It is for everyone who wants to remain pure for his or her future mate and wants to obey God's commandment to be holy. The reason more people don't avail themselves of this gift is they don't know of it, or they have trouble believing God. This is one of the ways I know God is real, and that He is true to His promises to give us power over all our enemies (even over our greatest enemy, self). I was enslaved by sexual lusts for over 25 years before God set me free. Then I lost my first wife to cancer and was single for 4 years prior to meeting and marrying my present wife. I can attest to the fact that the gift of celibacy is real and it works. God kept me from being caught up in sexual sins while waiting for Him to bring me my current wife.

There is a right way and a wrong way for men and women to meet, court, and become mates for life. The way the world views dating is asking for trouble. If you want to kiss and pet, you can kiss your gift of celibacy goodbye. When dating you should take your date to group affairs where each of you can get to know each other in safety. Dates where you are alone for extended periods of time should be withheld until you are sure you respect each other enough that you will not violate the other's trust. When going to places of entertainment, you should show discretion about choosing the type of entertainment you will partake of. The main thing is to recognize that everyone has a need to be loved, and we all fight a battle with loneliness. Don't place yourself in places where you are going to be tempted beyond your capability to resist. Sexual desires when stimulated can get out of our ability to control. You can't hold fire against your chest and not get burnt.

In my many years of working with those who are attempting to recover from chemical addictions, I have seen many suffer multiple relapses. In almost every instance I found that where they started to lose it was when they got involved in a wrong relationship. It wasn't long after they committed sexual acts that their ability to resist the temptation to use drugs was so eroded that they fell victim again to their addiction. Let's look at this: Does not the Word of God say, ***"The Wages of sin is death"*** (Romans 6:23)? When we disobey God we experience spiritual death. Spiritual death means separation from God, and the loss of His power. If it is God's power that is replacing our weakness, aren't we a pushover for the devil to get us back into our chemical addictions when we fall into sexual sins? If you struggle with sexual lust, you need to know that victory in this area will probably not come easy. This can be a real stronghold, but nothing is impossible with God. If God set this sinner free, He will do the same for you. After all, the Word says that He is no respecter of persons (Acts 10:34). What He does for one, He will do for all who seek His face.

It is written: *"But remember this-the wrong desires that come into your life aren't anything new and different. Many others have faced exactly the same problems before you. And no temptation is irresistible. You can trust God to keep the temptation from becoming so strong that you can't stand up against it, for He has promised this and will do what He says. He will show you how to escape temptation's power so that you can bear up patiently against it"* (1 Corinthians 10:13 LB). The problem of being set free from those sins that so easily beset us is not that God is not able; it is that we are weak in our faith. We simply don't believe that God is able to rescue us in our time of temptation, so we give up without a fight. Yes, we need to grow in faith, and we need to know about the spiritual warfare we are in and how to fight, but there is something else we need to know. In God's dealing with man, there is a duality of responsibility. There are some things you can do, and some things you can't do. Example: In our deliverance from the sins of sexual lust, we can stop looking at those things that would stimulate us sexually. Pornographic magazines, worldly television programs, etc.

And we can seek and find what the Word of God says about lust and sexual sin, and how we can involve ourselves in spiritual warfare so we can get God's mighty power working on our behalf. Then God will do for us those things we are incapable of doing. He will break the bondage that lust holds over us. He will strengthen us for the battle as we seek to break sinful habits. He says, *"Fear thou not; for I am with thee: be not dismayed; for I am thy God: I will strengthen thee; yea, I will help thee; yea, I will uphold thee with the right hand of my righteousness"* (Isaiah 41:10).

We teach a course in recovery programs and in prison on relationships, that shows how we have been programmed by Hollywood to do relationships the wrong way. Hollywood's formula: 1- Find the right person; 2 - Fall in love; 3 – Put all of your hopes, dreams, and aspirations in that person; 4 – When the relationship fails, go back and repeat steps one through three. This is a failed formula. Chip Ingram in his book: **Love, Sex, and Lasting Relationships** shows that God has a formula that works.

Chapter 10
Pain & Addiction

One of the main reasons people continue to indulge in sexual immorality, or abuse alcohol and drugs, in spite of the problems they cause, is they are attempting to <u>medicate their pain</u>. Most who have become involved in an addictive lifestyle are not aware of this. Loneliness, fear, rejection, and anger, are some of the pains people try to medicate. Anger is a major, major cause of pain. Has anyone ever pushed your buttons, causing you to become really angry? Have circumstances in your life caused you to feel frustrated and angry? Have memories of past abuse caused you to experience anger? I think we all can relate to those times when we have felt anger. Some find this emotion to be overwhelming at times, and some even seem to get stuck in anger. You should know this very important fact; **Anger is painful**. Anybody who experiences anger over an extended period of time will need to medicate the pain it causes. People use different ways of medicating. For some it's chemicals. For others it is promiscuous sex. For still others it is overeating. Whatever one uses to medicate their pain, it can be harmful both to them and to those with whom they are in close relationship. No one likes to experience pain. All of us seek some form of relief when we experience pain, regardless of whether it is physical or emotional pain. Those who have been caught up in an addictive lifestyle will reach for their usual painkiller even if logically they know that what they are doing to obtain some relief will cause them more pain in the future. Our immediate need to escape pain eliminates all of our logical reasons for not using our painkiller.

Fear is another emotion, which if not dealt with can be very painful. The problem with fear as well as with anger is that it often goes unrecognized. Most people, if asked, "Do you have any major fears?" would respond with a strong denial. Yet upon closer examination, they would have to admit there are times when they feel up tight or anxious for no apparent reason. Men especially have a problem getting in touch with their fears. It's part of their macho image. But honestly speaking, we all have fears. Are you fearful when you are out looking for work, and are about to enter a prospective employer's office? How about when you are going for an interview? How about if you are called upon to do any kind of public speaking? How about when you go to the dentist? Or when the doctor wants to give you a shot? I have seen some big burly men faint dead away when they saw that needle. Then there are the fears we experience every time

Pain & Addiction

we find ourselves around a certain type of person, or in a certain environment. Those times when the anxiety gets so strong we feel like saying, "Man I need a drink!" Those panic attacks can usually be traced to a time in our childhood when we were placed in danger or abused in some way. Often we have no recollection of these childhood events, but people, places, or events can trigger our subconscious memory. Then comes the anxiety attack, and with it, our need to medicate.

Those of us, who have come from broken families, or whose parents were substance abusers, often feel the pain of **rejection**. The pain of rejection can affect those whose parents worked so much that they weren't available when they needed them. Have you ever been through a divorce, or experienced the end of a meaningful relationship? Was the rejection you felt painful? It's those times that the loneliness becomes overwhelming! That's when we are tempted to medicate.

I have been working with recovering addicts since 1980. While I have seen many who have overcome their addictions, for some it was very difficult, with many relapses. I have pondered long and hard as to why someone who did so well in one of our programs would within a very short time find themselves once again in the grip of addiction. Thankfully with new knowledge about the causes and effects of addiction we have improved our percentage of those who have remained drug free. Still, some of our most promising clients would relapse. Why?

We are taking a closer look at the relationship between pain and addiction. We are learning new methods of assisting people to get in touch with the origin of their pain, so they can receive their healing. You see, it is not enough just to identify one's pain. You must get to the root of the pain. Too often we find those in the medical profession just treating symptoms rather than getting to the cause of their patients' distress. The medial field has a pill for everything, but these pills are only treating the symptoms. Unless you get at the root, you will be like the person trying to eradicate crabgrass by tearing off the shoots. Unless you dig it up by the roots, it will just come back again.

A definition for addiction: A pattern of thinking that leads to a pattern of behavior. The antidote. **Repentance**: Change your pattern of thinking.

In our work with ex-offenders we have had some success in using a teaching called **Inner Healing**. This enables a person to examine the correlation between spirit, soul, and body. The healing process begins in the soulish realm where our feelings originate. We are able to demonstrate how abuses in our childhood (physical, sexual, and emotional) caused deep imbedded memories of pain. Often these memories cause feelings of anger or fear to surface when triggered by current events. Many have been able to allow Jesus to revisit them at the origin of their woundedness and receive their healing.

Recently, we were introduced to another healing ministry that has tremendous promise in setting captives free.

Pain & Addiction

The reports we have heard show where many who have struggled for years with emotionally crippling illnesses have been set free in one or two sessions. One report dealt with a number of ladies in an **Adult Victims of Sexual Abuse** support group. After years of attempting to overcome the pain and ongoing dysfunction with only minimal success, many who participated in this new therapy reported their feelings of fear and anger completely gone. On follow up visits, months later, they reported no reoccurrence. **Dr. Ed Smith**, the founder of **Theophostic Prayer Ministry** (1) tells of a specific case where a man sought his help in dealing with homosexual temptations. He reported that he had accepted Christ as his Savior 15 years earlier and had remained abstinent since that time, but really struggled with these temptations. After one 45-minute session in which Dr. Smith took this man back to his childhood and dealt with a rape and other incidents that brought confusion about his sexual identity, the patient was able to experience a healing encounter with Jesus. The patient reported that for the first time in his life he felt completely free. Six months later this patient telephoned Dr. Smith to tell him that not once in all that time had he had a homosexual thought. He was completely free!

We recognize the potential this therapy has in helping anyone who wants freedom from their addiction. All of our staff are presently receiving training in this healing therapy. In spite of our limited experience with this concept we have already had some success with the first few people who have allowed us to work with them. Including members of our own staff. If this therapy measures up to its advance billing it could revolutionize recovery ministries. It could greatly shorten the time needed for the recovery process.

All of us experience pain, but most of us don't handle it very well. Pain is inevitable. Whether we want to or not, we had better learn how to deal with it. I used to think it was just a matter of learning how to do a better job of coping with our pains. However, now I believe there is a need to find the origin of our woundedness in order to receive our healing. Once that is accomplished we are in a much better position to deal with our current issues.

All of the teachings used by Theophostic Ministry are based on Scripture. The healing therapies utilized recognize that Jesus is the Healer, and we are just instruments He uses to bring people to Him so He can touch them. Our goal is to break the cycle of pain and addiction with its subsequent consequences. We want to do everything in our power to make our work more effective.

Chapter 11
Sex And Recovery Ministry

Let's consider how ones sexual activity affects the person who is seeking recovery from chemical addiction. As one who was addicted to both alcohol and sex I have a pretty good handle on this subject. Especially since I have been involved in helping those recovering from alcohol and drug addiction since 1980, and more recently to sex-offenders.

For 10 years I was the director of The Regeneration Center, a Christian recovery center in West Palm Beach, Florida. That program saw many of its client's set free of their addictions. However, one thing kept bothering me. Many of our graduates who showed great promise would fall victim again to their addiction. These were men who had been alcohol and drug free for many months. Yet, within a short time after leaving our program they would relapse. In our networking with other recovery programs I discovered that this trend occurred far too often. Why was this happening? My research revealed that in almost every case these men had become involved in a relationship outside of marriage. I concluded that this sexual liaison had caused them to lose fellowship with their Heavenly Father. This in turn caused them to lose the power He had given them to resist the temptation to drink and use drugs. I also discovered another shocking fact! Most programs, including ours, did not have a curriculum that dealt with topics concerning ones sexual appetite, and the consequences of involvement in adultery, fornication, and homosexuality.

Ignorance is not bliss! Hosea 4:6 says, **"My people are destroyed for lack of knowledge."** It amazes me that the church and ministries to recovering addicts fall short in informing those in their care of the dangers of uncontrolled sexual activity. How can this be, when the Scriptures clearly warn of the dangers of fornication and adultery? **"Don't fool yourselves. Those who live immoral lives, who are idol worshipers, adulterers or homosexuals - will have no share in His Kingdom. That is why I say to run from sex sin. No other sin affects the body as this one does."** (1 Corinthians 6:10, 18 LB) **"Let there be no sex sin, impurity or greed among you. Let no one be able to accuse you of any such things."** (Ephesians 5:3 LB) We have been brought up in a world system that tells us that anything goes when it comes to satisfying our sexual urges. Can we afford to ignore God's warnings? We need to know how vulnerable we are when it comes to our sexual drive, and learn God's way of dealing with it.

OUR SEXUALITY

Is our sexuality a gift from our Creator, or a curse? Few would consider their sexuality a curse. Those who have become enslaved to pornography and/or become involved in sexually immoral practices might. Those who have broken the law and been convicted of committing a sexual crime certainly would. But not everyone who has broken God's law with regards their sexual activities are conscious of the consequences resulting from their acts.

Let's look at this. We are well aware of the consequences of falling unto the long arm of the law! But there is a Higher Court from which none of us can escape! What are some of the consequences? Well, if you are married and cheat on your wife, you run the risk of losing her love and trust. Infidelity is a major cause of the breakup of the family. Even if you are not caught, you rob yourself and your mate of the close intimacy that is so necessary in a healthy marriage. Even sexual fantasy can greatly harm the intimacy between a man and his wife.

What about the single person who is acting out immorally? Does he/she suffer consequences? Yes, both in the natural and in the spiritual. In the natural, they are in danger of becoming addicted (enslaved) to their immoral activity. There are long-range consequences. The brain records those events and will replay them over and over again, causing one to be tempted to repeat their behavior, possibly later when they are married. In the spiritual realm, they will lose the close intimacy they need with their Heavenly Father. "The wages of sin is death!" (Romans 6:23a) When we break God's laws we become spiritually separated from God. This results in our losing His peace, and His power. If this happens at a time when we need Him to help us to overcome other weaknesses in our life (like recovery from alcoholism or drug addiction) the results can be devastating.

SEXUAL ADDICTION

Like most addictions, those who are addicted to sex often remain in denial. How can we identify sexual addiction, and how big a problem is it? I don't know of any surveys conducted on this issue, but it wouldn't surprise me to find that among men possibly 50% or more could be classified as addicts.

Would you like to take a test? Do you find yourself drawn to television programs that exploit a woman's sexual allure? Maybe you are drawn to magazines that show beautiful young ladies in various states of undress? Have you a problem with masturbation? You know it isn't right. You have tried numerous times to quit, but it has such a hold on you. You tell yourself you are not going to do that again, but there you are, back again. You feel so ashamed, but you just can't help yourself; so you begin to rationalize. Surely God understands ..... He knows what it's like..... He made me this way!

When the guilt gets too bad, we have to find a way out, even if it means blaming God! Tell me, has that worked? Has it taken away the guilt and shame? Has it made you feel close to God? I'm sure, if you are being honest with yourself, you'll admit that blaming God, or rationalizing the behavior doesn't work. God wants us to enjoy a close intimate relationship with Him. He desires to show us His glory, but how can a Holy God draw close to someone who is lustful? When you see a pretty girl, where do your eyes go? What are your thoughts? I know that before I decided to make the Lord my Master my eyes would be drawn to a woman's body. Then I would entertain thoughts of being sexually intimate with her. Before you condemn me as being a sexual pervert, think, didn't I have a lot of company? The majority of men would say, as long as I didn't act out on those thoughts I was okay. There are two problems with this line of thinking. Was I okay in God's eyes? Then there is this problem: "Sow a thought, reap an action." When we who are creatures of habit dwell on these kinds of thoughts, a time will come when we will act upon them. I know that in my own life I became addicted to pornography at a young age. This led to a stronghold of masturbation and infidelity in my marriage. Chasing after women contributed to my alcoholism.

HOW DOES ONE BECOME ADDICTED TO SEX?

It is normal for children as they come into puberty, to become aware of their sexuality and begin to experiment. Many of us learn very early in life how to give ourselves pleasure sexually.

Since there is a part of our brain that causes us to return to those activities that gave us feelings of pleasure, it is easy to become addicted to those feelings. Once that happens, we are hooked. The same neurotransmitters in our brain that release endorphins that cause some to become addicted to alcohol or cocaine are activated when we are stimulated sexually. We literally program our brain to activate these endorphins when certain events or circumstances trigger the brain. Thus, our thought life can become our biggest enemy. It triggers our brain to release those endorphins.

Often our failures happen through our thought life. *For as he thinketh in his heart, so is he.* (Proverbs 27:3a) Our thought life governs our actions. "Sow a thought, reap an action. Sow an action, reap a habit. Sow a habit, reap a lifestyle." *Be not deceived; God is not mocked: for whatsoever a man soweth, that shall he also reap. For he that soweth to his flesh shall of the flesh reap corruption; but he that soweth to the Spirit shall of the Spirit reap life everlasting.* (Galatians 6:7, 8)

First we identified the problem. It's lust! *"I tell you that anyone who looks at a woman lustfully has already committed adultery with her in his heart."* (Matthew 5:28) *"Keep thy heart with all diligence, for out of it are the issues of life."* (Proverbs 4:23)

Identifying the problem is easy. Learning to be an "overcomer" will require more effort. In order to win the victory in this area; we are going to need God's help. This is a problem of the flesh, and if we try to overcome it in our own strength, we will fail. Flesh warring against flesh will lose every time. If lust has become a stronghold in our lives, we will need God's power to break that stronghold.

How can we get God's help? Well, if you have not been "born again" of His Spirit you can't. Your sins have separated you from God. A Holy God will not place Himself in the presence of sin. So then, we must recognize our need and want to turn from sin to God. Then we must believe that God placed the penalty for our sins upon Jesus. That He died on the Cross for our sins, and that He rose from the dead, conquering sin and death. The Bible says that if you will confess with your mouth Jesus as your lord and believe in your heart that God raised Him from the dead, you will be saved. (Romans 10:9) When we do that and mean it with all our heart, God takes our sins (every one of them) and casts them as far as the east is from the west. He casts them into a sea of forgetfulness, never to be remembered anymore. Then He takes that which was dead (us), and causes us to come alive in Him. He uses that same mighty power that He used to raise Christ from the dead. ***But if the Spirit of him that raised up Jesus from the dead dwell in you, he that raised up Christ from the dead shall also quicken your mortal bodies by his Spirit that dwelleth in you.*** (Romans 8:11) That word "quicken" means "to come alive". ***And what is the exceeding greatness of his power to us-ward who believe, according to the working of his mighty power, which he wrought in Christ, when he raised him from the dead, and set him at his own right***

hand in the heavenly places. Ephesians 1:19, 20) When one is born again, he becomes the righteousness of God in Christ. He literally becomes one with Christ, the Righteous One.

Becoming one with God does not automatically deliver one from the "bondage" of sin. There are many Christians who struggle with addiction problems. Everyone should pray this prayer: **Search me, O God, and know my heart: try me, and know my thoughts: And see if there be any wicked way in me, and lead me in the way everlasting.** (Psalms 139:23, 24) Now you have given God permission to help you to overcome in your areas of weakness. **He sent his <u>word</u>, and healed them, and delivered them from their <u>destructions</u>.** (Psalms 107:20)

2 Corinthians 10:3-5 says, *"For though we walk in the flesh, we do not war after the flesh: For the weapons of our warfare are not carnal, but mighty through God to the <u>pulling down of strongholds</u>; <u>Casting down imaginations</u> and every high thing that exalteth itself against the knowledge of God, and <u>bringing into captivity every thought</u> to the obedience of Christ."* Did you get that? We don't war in our flesh, but using God's mighty weapons we are able to pull down strongholds and imaginations, and bring our thought life into obedience to Christ.

Before Alcoholics Anonymous the general consensus was: "Once a drunk, always a drunk". Now it is generally accepted that alcoholism is a disease and its victims can be healed. Fifty years from now the public will know that sexual addicts can be healed of their addiction. When you took your test on sexual addiction, did you detect a problem? If so, <u>do you want to be healed</u>? Then look unto God's Word; *"My son, attend to my words; incline thine ear unto my sayings. Let them not depart from thine eyes; keep them in the midst of thine heart. For they are life unto those that find them, and health to all their flesh."* (Proverbs 4:20-22) For they are <u>life</u> to them that find them, and <u>healing</u> to all their <u>flesh</u>. *Thy Word have I hid in mine heart, that I might not sin against thee."* (Psalms 119:6)

Two Scripture passages that helped to set me free of my sexual addiction were Philippians 4:8 and Job 31:1. The one deals with our thought life and the other with our roving eye. Philippians 4:8: *"Finally, brethren, whatsoever things are true, whatsoever things are honest, whatsoever things are just, whatsoever things are pure, whatsoever things are lovely, whatsoever things are of good report; if there be any virtue, and if there be any praise, think on these things."* We are to focus our thoughts on those things that are honest and true, and sexually pure. We are to avoid negative reports and concentrate on good reports. *"For as he thinketh in his heart, so is he."* (Proverbs 23:7a) It won't be easy to break a habit of thinking impure or negative thoughts, but with God's help you will succeed. Remember the best way to break an old habit, is to replace it with a new habit. If you do something consistently for 30 days, it will

The Modern Day Leper

become a habit. Every time you find yourself thinking wrong thoughts, replace them with the Word that you have hid in your heart (memorized).

Job 31:1LB: *"I made a covenant with my eyes not to look with lust upon a girl."* This was the Scripture that brought conviction that I was sinning with my eyes. I said; "Wow Lord, I'll make that same covenant that Job made." After I had done that, whenever I would see a girl I was attracted to, I would remind myself of my covenant. So, instead of allowing my eyes to traverse to what would make me lust, I would look upon her face, even looking into her eyes. I also would remind myself that she was someone's daughter, and someone our heavenly Father loved. I would remind myself that she was not just a physical being, but that she also possessed a spirit and a soul. I became interested in her as an intellectual person and I was concerned as to how she was spiritually connected to Father God. In the past, when I was undressing her with my eyes, I eliminated any chance that I might have had to share my faith with her. Stephen Arterburn's book **Every Man's Battle** is a wonderful resource for overcoming sexual lust. As is Steve Gallagher's **At the Alter of Sexual Idolatry**.

The Scripture verses in this chapter go a long way to setting one free of sexual lust and addiction. However, I have learned through years of assisting recovering addicts that it is necessary to minister to the total person. We are not just spiritual beings, so we must also address those issues that deal with the body and soul. Our soul has to do with our mind, will and emotions. Oftentimes events that occurred in our past have caused our mind and will to be bent in a certain direction. Also past events may have caused damage to our emotions. Since we tend to act on our feelings, it is important that we find out what causes us to feel certain things. This cannot be dealt with without personal counseling. Those who are in a recovery program are usually exposed to counseling dealing with "Inner Healing" or "Healing of Damaged Emotions." If you need help in this area, find out if these sessions are offered at a local church. If you do avail yourself of this type of counseling, it is important that you trust your counselor and not try to control the counseling sessions. This is covered more fully in chapter ten, Pain & Addiction.

Now we are going to take a look at one of the most perplexing things facing today's sex offenders! How can they cope with all the fear and hostility they are facing?

I have good news and bad news. The good news is that no matter how bad things may appear, there is a place of refuge, a place where we can run to receive protection. It is in the arms of God. The things of this world cannot satisfy, nor can they afford us safety. The good news is that God loves you and has a bright future for you. Jeremiah 29:11LB says: *For I know the plans I have for you, says the Lord. They are plans for good and not for evil, to give you a*

future and a hope. The good news is that God's plans for those who are rightly related to Him are for good and not for evil, and He is big enough and bad enough to back up His plans. The bad news is that for those who are not rightly related to Him, He has no obligation to fulfill this Scripture for them.

Chapter 12
Justice For All

What has happened to our judicial system? Most people assume that someone accused of a crime in the United States is afforded all the protection the constitution decrees. That he or she is innocent until proven guilty. That if he or she cannot afford an attorney, one will be provided them.

All that is true according to our laws, but there is not equal justice for all. Those who cannot afford the high price tag for a private attorney will be represented by a "Public Defender." Sounds great, but there are problems within the system. One of the problems is that the attorney from the public defenders office is actually an employee of the state. The state is the entity that is prosecuting the accused. Add to this the fact that the public defender is given such a huge case load that he/she cannot possibly give a prepared defense to any but the highest profile cases and very few of them.

What generally happens is the prosecuting attorney will develop a case using the worst possible scenario. Whether the evidence supports it or not, he will charge the accused with as many felonies as possible so that if convicted of all the charges the accused is looking at a sentence of 20, 30, 40 or more years.

Those in jail who cannot afford to post bail often are forced to cool their heels for several months before they receive a visit from their public defender who informs them concerning the charges against them and the gravity of their situation. This attorney will most likely suggest that a deal can be brokered with the prosecuting attorney where some of the charges will be dropped resulting in a reduced sentence, if the accused will plead guilty. This is referred to as a **"plea bargain."**

What you now have is someone who is not representing the best interest of the accused, but someone who is really a lackey of the prosecuting attorney. Prosecuting attorneys are notorious for having the attitude that every defendant is guilty as charged and is deserving of the most severe sentence the law will allow. Now enters the public defender as he attempts to convince the accused to plead guilty or face the possibility of spending the rest of their natural life in prison. Rather than pursuing how they can best defend the accused they usually present how the prosecutor has such a strong case against them, that they would be foolish taking their case to trial and risk receiving the larger sentence. That is why the majority of the public defender's cases are settled via the plea bargain route.

Justice For All

Are there innocent people in prison? I have conversed with many who were charged with molesting a minor that were told if they didn't plead out they would most certainly be convicted, since the jury would believe the testimony of a child as opposed to their testimony. There are those who were under the influence of alcohol or drugs and don't even remember the events that were alleged to have occurred with regards the crimes for which they are accused. There are others whose mental and emotional state while awaiting trial was such that they could not make reasonable decisions when being pressured to accept a plea bargain. I believe there are men and women in prison who shouldn't be there, and there are those who have received sentences far in excess of the crimes they committed.

It should be noted that once a person agrees to a plea bargain, they lose any right of appeal with regards their conviction or the sentence they receive. Our judicial system gives a convicted defendant the right to appeal their conviction or the length of their sentence if they can show sufficient cause for these things to be reviewed. This is not so if they agree to a plea bargain. This means, when they recover from the emotional shock of all that has transpired and realize they have made a mistake in accepting the plea, there is no way of trying to correct it. There are men and women in prison serving long sentences that know they should never have given up their right of appeal. Usually this is not explained to them when the public defender convinces them to accept a plea bargain. Chapter seven gives an example of what can happen to one who accepts a plea bargain.

The Modern Day Leper

When we recite the pledge of allegiance to the flag of the Unites States, we end it with the phrase, "With Liberty and Justice for All." I long for the day that those words would be true.

One of the greatest testimonies to be brought to the House Judiciary Committee was brought by the father of Rachel Scott, one of 12 students killed at the Columbine High School massacre in Littleton, Colorado. I enclose it here for your consideration:

Darrell Scott, the father of Rachel Scott, a victim of the Columbine High School shootings in Littleton, Colorado, was invited to address the House Judiciary Committee's sub-committee.

What he said to our national leaders during this special session of Congress was painfully truthful. They were not prepared for what he was to say, nor was it received well. It needs to be heard by every parent, every teacher, every politician, every sociologist, every psychologist, and every so-called expert!

These courageous words spoken by Darrell Scott are powerful, penetrating, and deeply personal. There is no doubt that God sent this man as a voice crying in the wilderness. The following is a portion of the Transcript:

"Since the dawn of creation there has been both good & evil in the hearts of men and women. We all contain the

seeds of kindness or the seeds of violence. The death of my wonderful daughter, Rachel Joy Scott, and the deaths of that heroic teacher, and the other eleven children who died must not be in vain. Their blood cries out for answers."
"The first recorded act of violence was when Cain slew his brother Abel out in the field. The villain was not the club he used. Neither was it the NCA, the National Club Association. The true killer was Cain, and the reason for the murder could only be found in Cain's heart. "In the days that followed the Columbine tragedy, I was amazed at how quickly fingers began to be pointed at groups such as the NRA. I am not a member of the NRA. I am not a hunter. I do not even own a gun. I am not here to represent or defend the NRA - because I don't believe that they are responsible for my daughter's death. Therefore I do not believe that they need to be defended. If I believed they had anything to do with Rachel's murder I would be their strongest opponent."

"I am here today to declare that Columbine was not just a tragedy-it was a spiritual event that should be forcing us to look at where the real blame lies! Much of the blame lies here in this room. I wrote a poem that expresses my feelings best. This was written way before I knew I would be speaking here today:"

> Your laws ignore our deepest needs,
> Your words are empty air.
> You've stripped away our heritage,
> You've outlawed simple prayer.

> Now gunshots fill our classrooms,
> And precious children die.
> You seek for answers everywhere,
> And ask the question "Why?"
>
> You regulate restrictive laws,
> Through legislative creed.
> And yet you fail to understand,
> That God is what we need!

"Men and women are three-part beings. We all consist of body, soul, and spirit. When we refuse to acknowledge a third part of our make-up, we create a void that allows evil, prejudice, and hatred to rush in and reek havoc. Spiritual influences were present within our educational systems for most of our nation's history. Many of our major colleges began as theological seminaries. This is a historical fact. What has happened to us as a nation? We have refused to honor God, and in so doing, we open the doors to hatred and violence. And when something as terrible as Columbine's tragedy occurs politicians immediately look for a scapegoat such as the NRA. They immediately seek to pass more restrictive laws that contribute to erode away our personal and private liberties.

We do not need more restrictive laws." Eric and Dylan would not have been stopped by metal detectors. No amount of gun laws can stop someone who spends months planning this type of massacre. The real villain lies within our own hearts. Political posturing and restrictive legislation are not the answers. The young people of our nation hold the key. There is a spiritual awakening taking place that will not be squelched! We do not need more religion. We do not need more gaudy television evangelists spewing out verbal religious garbage. We do not need more million dollar church buildings built while people with basic needs are being ignored. We do need a change of heart and a humble acknowledgment that this nation was founded on the principle of simple trust in God! As my son Craig lay under that table in the school library and saw his two friends murdered before his very eyes, He did not hesitate to pray in school. "I defy any law or politician to deny him that right."

"I challenge every young person in America, and around the world, to realize that on April 20, 1999, at Columbine High School prayer was brought back to our schools. Do not let the many prayers offered by those students be in vain. Dare to move into the new millennium with a sacred disregard for legislation that violates your God-given right to communicate with Him. To those of you who would point your finger at the NRA- I give to you a sincere challenge. Dare to examine your own heart before casting the first stone! My daughter's death will not be in vain! The young people of this country will not allow that to happen!"

Chapter 13
Prejudice

The United States has always had a problem with prejudice and discrimination. We have always had our "whipping boy". In our early history it was the Negro and slavery. During the Second World War we sent thousands of Japanese citizens into concentration camps. Today the sex offender is the one we shower with prejudice and discrimination. Often our first impressions can be wrong. Open communication, however, can correct misunderstandings that are created by our own pride and prejudice. Rather than believing everything we hear about sex offenders, wouldn't it be wise to do a little investigating in an attempt to learn what is true and what is fable? Those who work with sex offenders are often willing to dialogue with those who are seeking honest answers. Since first impressions often lead to wrong conclusions, let's get beyond that and dig a little deeper. If you do, you will find that not many charged with a sexual crime are a monster, but that every case is different and each individual is different. To be sure, there are those who should be feared, but most can be assimilated into our communities without endangering our children or us.

Prejudice: Reader's Digest Encyclopedic Dictionary

1- A judgment or opinion formed beforehand or without thoughtful examination of the pertinent facts, issues, or arguments; especially, an unfavorable, irrational opinion.
2- The act or state of holding pre-conceived, irrational opinions.
3- Hatred of or dislike for a particular group, race, religion, etc.
4- Injury or damage to a person arising from a hasty and unfair judgment by others.

Looking at the dictionary definition of prejudice, we see that it is predicated on a judgment or opinion made without thoughtful examination of the pertinent facts, issues, or arguments; <u>especially an unfavorable, irrational opinion</u>.

Lay this definition over how we are currently dealing with those who have been convicted of sexual crimes and it is apparent that we have not learned very much with the passing of time. As we have pointed out in earlier chapters, the laws we have passed regarding sex offenders have not been based on facts pertaining to their being a possible ongoing threat, or their being apt to re-offend. Studies have clearly shown that only one to three percent of sex offenders are pedophiles, and that between 87 and 94 percent of those who serve prison time for sex crimes do not re-offend. Still the laws our legislators have passed are based on the most serious of offenders and all sex offenders are forced to obey them.

"Prejudice and discrimination are deeply imbedded at both the individual and societal levels. Attempts to eradicate prejudice and discrimination must thus deal with prevailing beliefs, ideologies and social structure. As to the root cause of prejudice and discrimination there appears to be no clear evidence of any theory of causation. Scholars do agree, however, that prejudice and discrimination are not universal as something humans are inherently born with. There is ample evidence that prejudice and discrimination are social constructions. Although there is no wide agreement as to the "cause" of prejudice and discrimination, there is a consensus that they constitute a learned behavior. The media and social institutions solidify prejudicial attitudes, giving them legitimacy. The most overlooked area in resolving the problems of prejudice and discrimination lies in the web of close relationships where genuine feelings of love can be fostered and strengthened. The private sphere may indeed be the last frontier where a solution to the problems of prejudice may have to be found. Prejudice and discrimination produce immense effects in the psychological, social, political, and economic domains. Whether intended or not, the effects are compounded by the loss of self-worth, a sense of alienation from the wider society, political disempowerment, and economic inequalities. Just as it is humanity's capacity to create prejudice and discrimination, it is also within its capacity to eradicate them. Prejudice and discrimination lead to disunity, which results in the dissolving of society through strife and war. World peace will elude our grasp while prejudice and discrimination continue to bedevil the collective life of humanity". (1)

Truly prejudice and discrimination of sex offenders is a learned behavior that the media has solidified through their habit of sensationalizing the most horrific crimes.

Chapter 14
Fear

In today's world there are many problems that produce fear and guilt in the lives of people. The resulting stress becomes at times, unbearable. In America fear is everywhere. We are taught to fear terrorist attacks, high prices, a stock market crash, sex-offenders, and all kinds of health issues, from cancer to obesity. Why do we have such an obsession with fear? It should come as no surprise that there is an unseen enemy sowing fear in the hearts of people. In fact, fear is the most powerful weapon in the devil's arsenal. It keeps us from trying new things. It keeps us from developing new relationships. It even keeps us from exploring new opportunities to improve our standard of living, and it causes us to pre-judge, to be suspicious, and to be critical of others.

The Modern Day Leper

Fear is addictive. The body experiences an adrenaline rush that is as addicting as any drug. It feels good to be scared, as any bungee jumper will attest to when, after completing his plummet, exclaims, "What a rush!" But fear is usually not a good thing. When we are afraid, we are not at peace. Fear creates a turmoil and chaos in our lives and contributes to ailments such as migraines, panic attacks, high blood pressure, and depression. The human body is not meant to live in a state of fear. Adrenaline was programmed for emergency situations only. Yet people are purposely subjecting themselves to fear and anxiety situations every single day. It is no wonder our health suffers.

FEAR:

False
Evidence
Appearing
Real

If you are dealing with fears and insecurities from old head programs, have compassion on yourself. Just love your insecurities, fears and resentments. Release and forgive them as they come up. Judging, beating or repressing insecurities just gives them power. You then have a pattern that rarely gets resolved. Recognize that your real security is built from your relationship with your own heart.

Quotes of the Heart:

Japanese proverb: ***Fear is only as deep as the mind allows.***

Napoleon: ***He who fears being conquered is sure of defeat.***

Marie Curie: ***Nothing in life is to be feared. It is only to be understood.***

Bryon Janis: ***Fear breeds fear.***

Franklin D. Roosevelt: ***The only thing we have to fear is fear itself.***

Michael Pritchard: ***Fear is that little darkroom where negatives are developed.*** (1)

The antidote for fear is faith! But faith in what? The only type of faith that will bring real relief from fear is "Faith in God!" One of renowned Evangelist R.W. Shambach's famous statements is: "You don't have any problems. All you need is, **Faith in God**."

II Timothy 1:7 points this out: "God has not given us the spirit of fear, but of power, and love, and of a sound mind." The spirit of fear comes from Satan who uses it to keep us down and defeated. God has given us the spirit of power to live constructively, the spirit of love to live sacrificially, and a sound mind to live reasonably.

In today's world there are many problems that produce fear and guilt in the lives of people. The resulting stress is at times, unbearable, and may ultimately lead to emotional breakdowns and physical problems. We were never created to live under these kinds of problems. If we cannot handle this kind of stress, why are we so willing to place it upon some of our most vulnerable citizens?

The very people who are supposed to be helping sex offenders, their probation officers, are often harassing those who have served their prison sentences and are trying to make it back into society with little or no resources. The job description for a probation officer is to help the probationer in finding housing and employment. Instead, we see many of them using all manner of threats and other hindering tactics. This causes the probationer to break and do something that would violate the conditions of his or her probation, which would in turn send them back to prison.

Making matters worse is the outcry of people when a sex offender moves into a neighborhood. It is no surprise that the general populace has such a fear of sex offenders. The news media has created fear in the hearts of people with their sensationalizing sex crimes in the evening news. We are so quick to pre-judge others. When we get the news that one of these "sex offenders" is moving into our neighborhood, most are up in arms in protest. But, did they try to meet the new neighbor in an effort to determine if he or she is indeed a threat? Did they do anything to determine what he or she was charged with? Did they find out how long they were in prison, and what they are doing to see that they don't repeat their mistakes? Or, did they let their fears dictate their attitude towards their new neighbor?

Billy Graham once said, "Courage is contagious. When a brave man takes a stand, the spines of others are stiffened".

It is my prayer that this book will cause many to get the backbone to stand against the fear mongers and say, "I will not pre-judge my neighbor, but I will follow the commandment of our Lord to love my neighbor". At the very least, I will make a diligent effort to determine if there are any grounds for concern.

Chapter 15
By His Love

"Compassionate, Merciful, Kind, and Forgiving". These qualities describe our loving Lord and He said these same qualities would describe His own. God's word states that His children would have <u>His</u> heart, <u>His</u> focus, and <u>His</u> agenda. They will not live for themselves but will die daily and will allow Him to live through them. He said they will love Him with all their heart, mind, soul, and strength, and they will love others the way He loved them.

We have a whole segment of society that are screaming for help with almost no one coming to their aid. Who are these people? They are those who were caught in sexual sins and are now labeled as "sexual offenders". So many of these people have repented for their past failures and are desperately looking for someone to help them get their lives together and start on a new path. Sadly, their cries for help are falling on deaf ears. So, we have to ask ourselves, "Where is God's heart in all this?" God's word shows His heart. Look at those who have gone from death to life. Look at Rahab the harlot, David, Samson, Hosea's wife Gomer, the lady caught in adultery, and the woman at the well. Here we see the Lord's heart. All these were "sexual offenders". They repented and reflect how God's mercy and grace extends to those who come to Him.

Now, there are those whom God has raised up to be on the front lines, offering to help sex offenders deal with the hardships of living in a hostile environment. Those He has put face-to-face with the sexual offenders to extend His healing hand and His accepting heart toward the ones who have <u>repented</u> and <u>are asking for help</u>. Where do these ministers go to get the resources, finances, manpower, and other needed support? They turn and plead to the church for help. But, often they are met with deaf ears as even the mention of the words "sexual offender" brings a prejudice, and irrational hatred, that lack of knowledge has so cleverly formed in the minds and hearts of many, even church leaders.

So, what do we do with these people caught in this miry clay? Will not Christ remind us of His examples? How He went to the rejects, the cast outs, and those so despised by society. How He turned His back on Pharisaic Simon and embraced the one who had anointed His feet with tears and oil. Will He not ask why our hearts did not beat one with His towards those who were hurting and were so badly wounded? But some would say, "These sexual offenders have hurt children. How can we love and forgive them?" One only needs to look at 2 Chronicles 33 where we read about King Manasseh who was forgiven and restored to his kingdom after he had offered his own children as a sacrifice to a false god. God saw his repentive heart and showed him His mercy.

The Lord knows us by our works. Those who are His will reach out with a true heart and give these fallen ones the helping hand they need, or at least support those who are helping them. For Christ said, "I was thirsty, and ye gave me drink: naked and ye clothed me: I was sick, and you visited me: I was in prison and ye came unto me." (Matthew 25:35b-36b)

Two spirits are at work here in the world. Our faith shown by our works, will loudly declare to all who look at us, whose we really are. The strength of steel is determined under a big load and so is love. Our actions will show if our hearts beat with His. The Holy Spirit will do His office work, when we give Him office space! We are known by our love!

Chapter 16
For Parents

This book would not be complete without providing information for parents on how to protect your children from becoming a victim of any improper sex related incident. The biggest concern is that your child will be violated by a child molester whom you do not know. Chapter six points out that this is not likely to happen, but rather suggests that the biggest threat to your child being violated comes from within the family or close friends. The greater danger is that without proper training regarding their own sexuality your child may become involved in unhealthy sexual activities and end up victimizing another child. If that happens then your child runs the risk of being labeled a sex offender and will be faced with all the problems confronting sex offenders as outlined in this book.

That is the worse scenario; however that isn't the only danger. Without proper teaching on how to use the sexual gift our Creator has endowed us with, many have become sexually dysfunctional both as married couples and as singles. Each of us were created as sexual beings, and been given strong sexual drives. If we don't learn how God intended us to use those sexual drives, we can be headed for big trouble. We learned early in life how to give ourselves sexual pleasure and far too many have continued to seek those pleasures throughout their lives with little or no regard as to how they impacted the lives of others. The natural tendency of our flesh is for self gratification and probably nowhere is this more evident than in our sex life. Because of this, we see far too many marriages ending up in divorce, not to mention all the broken hearts of singles involved in relationships. Of course there are many other issues that can lead to the breakup of relationships, but sexual dysfunction is way up at the top. This is covered in detail in chapter eleven under the heading **"Our Sexuality."**

If you as a parent have never received good teaching on your sexuality, how can you teach your children? You can't give them something you don't have. I implore you to do some research on this subject. Some of the books I recommend are. **"Love, Sex & Lasting Relationships,"** by Chip Ingram (1); The **"Every Man's Battle"** series, by Stephen Arterburn and Fred Stoeker (2); and Pam Stenzel's video, **"Sex Has a Price Tag"** (3).

References: **1: Living on the Edge**
4201 N. Peachtree Road
Atlanta, GA 30341
www.lote.org

2: New Life Ministries
P.O. Box 1018
Laguna Beach, CA 92652
www.newlife.com

3: Enlighten Communications, Inc.
P.O. Box 270236
Littleton, CA 80127
www.pamstenzel.com

Chapter 17
For Pastors

The concern of many pastors is; how do I respond when a known sex offender wants to worship at our church? This is a legitimate concern, for it can be the source of great consternation among some members of your congregation, especially those who have been a victim of any type of molestation. Having read the book "A Time To Heal" by Rev. Debra Haffner I see no need to cover this subject. Rev. Haffner covers this subject in much greater detail than I could. She is the director of the Religious Institute on Sexual Morality, Justice and Healing. Her book contains the following forms:

Model Screening Form for Religious Educators & Youth Group Staff
Model Agreement to Teach

Model Limited Access Agreement
This latter form is one that the convicted sex offender would be expected to sign and abide by its conditions if he wants to worship with your congregation.
You may obtain a copy of her book by writing:
Religious Institute on Sexual Morality, Justice and Healing
304 Main Avenue, #335 Norwalk, CT 06851
www.religiousinstitute.org.

COVENANT OF GRACE

As believers in the redemptive power of the Cross we want to see God glorified through the representing of His love. Seeking to follow God's commandment to "love your neighbor as yourself" brings us to the humble consideration of how we would want to be treated if we ourselves had been publicly caught in sexual sin. We realize that Christ came to heal the sick and that His Church is called to be the spiritual hospital for those broken in spirit.

Boundaries for registered sex offenders(RSO's)
We realize that healthy boundaries protect and honor every one involved in the church. Guidelines for interaction and activities in the church should be determined on an individual basis since every RSO has different issues. We should consider each individuals own vulnerability and need for accountability. In view of this pastors may want to have a RSO complete the following survey:

For Pastors

Covenant Survey

All information will be held in confidence

Name: _____ Address: _____
Contact Phone:_ Home _____ Cell _____
Vehicle-Make: _____ Model: _____ Year: _____
Color: _____

Spiritual History

Are you a Christian?   Do you have a mentor?
   Y___N___   Y___N___

How did you come to know the Lord? _____
_____
_____

How has this relationship changed your life?
_____
_____
_____

Mentor's Name_____ Contact Phone _____
_____

Family History

Marital status: Married Divorced Single Separated (circle)
Children: How many? Male____ Female____ Number under 18 yr_____
Who do they live with? _____
Do you have visitation rights or custody? Y__ N__
Do you have emotional support from your family? Y__ N__

Criminal History

On the *back of this survey* please write a brief description of your criminal history including charges, time served, present status regarding parole or probation and information regarding name and contact #'s of Probation/Parole or Treatment Facilitator that we can contact regarding your status.

Treatment History

Are you currently in treatment? Y___ N___ How long?____
Treatment provider's name _____
Contact information: _____

REGISTRATION RECEIPT INFORMATION

Name of registering agency: _____
Contact name and #: _____
Registering Agency ORI: _____

Date of registration:_____
Registration #: _____ Next appt. date: _____

Criminal History

Charge/Conviction: (number of counts)

Brief Detail of Crime:

Number of Victims: _____ Victims Known: Y_____ N_____

Time Served:

Present Status:

Risk Level: Low Medium High (circle) Other: _____

Probation or Parole Officer/ District

Contact Phone:

EPILOGUE

It may be of interest to know that the author of this book and the character described in chapter two, titled "Case Study", are one and the same. The information contained there is accurate, except for what happened after I asked the judge for permission to marry my pregnant girlfriend. The judge let it be known that he could give me a 5-year prison sentence, but then decided to grant us permission to marry, so I never went to prison.

Although I was messed up then, I eventually got my act together. My wife and I were married for 25-years before she passed away in 1979. Shortly after her death I entered the ministry where I have been faithful to serve since 1980. I reveal this to let the reader know that many make mistakes, but given the chance, can go on to live productive lives.

What a difference 50 years can make. In 1953 the charge would have been statutory rape and would have carried a maximum sentence of 5 years. In today's society, the charge would be sexual battery on a minor under 16 and the maximum sentence would be 25 years plus 10 years probation. Today's judge would not have the liberty my judge had. Anyone charged with that same crime today would likely go to prison for a long, long time.

What has made the difference? Is the offence any more serious today than it was back then? Or is it that there has been such an increase in these types of crimes that stronger

The Modern Day Leper

sentences were mandated as a deterrent? The answer to both these questions is "no". Sexual activity between older men and younger girls has always gone on, and always will. Longer prison terms will probably not cause a decrease in this behavior. The difference is, television has become so mainstream in our society and the networks, in their competing with one another, will go to any length to get viewers. They don't care that sensationalizing news events has a downside. They learned that the public feeds on the sensational aspects of sexual crimes and they have taken this to a higher level. The result has been a groundswell of public disgust with anyone charged with a sexual crime. This has led politicians to pass stronger and stronger laws with regards to all sex crimes.

Our prisons in Florida as in many other states are called "Correctional Institutions". <u>The reality is they are not doing much to correct anything</u>. Most institutions are strictly punitive in nature. The result is that three out of every four released inmates are back in prison within five years.

There is a move to have our justice department consider "Restorative Justice". Former Chaplain Emmett Solomon who worked for four decades with the Texas Department of Criminal Justice is a leader in this movement. So is Chuck Colson's "Prison Fellowship".

Restorative Justice is a victim-focused approach to criminal justice. It encourages offenders to reflect on the harm caused by their criminal activity and to make restitution to victims,

Epilogue

the community and their families. It encourages offenders to participate in practices that are "restorative" in nature. These are designed to help offenders understand the impact of their behavior, accept responsibility for their actions, express remorse and take action to repair the damage. It provides victims a safe and structured opportunity to talk about the impact of crime on their lives. It also assists in developing in offenders an increased sensitivity towards victims that might prevent further victimization in the future. The offenders are compelled to explore the impact of their crimes on relationships in the community and within the families of the victims. Offenders are expected to develop respect for the rights of others and to become accountable for their actions.

A May 30, 2003 article in the "National Catholic Reporter" says, *"The adversary system discourages defendants from being active and outspoken. It dissuades them from expressing remorse or meeting with the victim. Often it creates in the defendant the feeling that he/she is the real victim, which is altogether accurate in a minority of cases, but feeds into many offenders tendency to deny the seriousness of the harm they've done their victims. Little wonder that many in both groups – victims and offenders alike – feel that the court process is not about them, but rather, that it is run for the convenience and interests of lawyers and judges."*

An article on the website of "Turning Point Partners" titled "**Turning Toward Compassion**: **Restorative Justice**

works to develop youths conscience" says, *"About 1,400 organizations nationwide are currently using the restorative justice method. So far, it has proven successful by reducing the recidivism rate by thirty two percent."* Finally, something that is showing promise in reducing the numbers of those returning to prison.

Why aren't we seeing more of our courts putting it into practice? Because we have become stuck in the punitive mold. "Make the one committing a crime pay, and give him/her as much time as possible to regret what they have done". This is so non-productive, that it is ludicrous. We have even gone so far as to take away much of the gain time prisoners could earn for good behavior. Now they must serve at least 85% of their sentence regardless of whether or not they are model prisoners. That, coupled with the longer sentences being given for almost all manner of crimes is swelling our prison population. In chapter five I point out how our prison population has swelled to over two million presently incarcerated. That direct and indirect cost of crime in America today is a staggering $193 billion per year and rising. These spiraling costs will eventually bankrupt our nation if we don't find a way to turn things around.

This book is about what I feel is the absolutely wrong way of dealing with those who have been charged with, and found guilty of committing a sexual crime. This book is about those who have served their prison sentence, but are being

Epilogue

hounded and harassed once they are released. Now, I want to let you know why I have chosen to try and assist them.

WHY HELP SEX OFFENDERS?

Because studies have shown that a sex addict <u>can</u> recover from his/her addiction. Our experience in operating a recovery program for sex offenders has also proven this to be true.

Because it is the right thing to do. ***"As we have therefore opportunity, let us do good unto all men, especially unto them who are of the household of faith".*** (Galatians 6:10) Too many who name the name of Christ have turned their back on these modern day lepers, but God hasn't. Jesus love is all-inclusive, never exclusive. It seems in fact, that He pours even more love on these that society excludes.

Why would anyone want to go against public opinion and try to assist sex offenders in their efforts to integrate into our communities upon completion of their prison sentences?

Why would anyone continue to help when opposition comes from everywhere and others who have tried to help have been forced to throw in the towel?

Because, statistics don't lie! We can't abandon those who have done their time and want the opportunity to live a normal life. Besides, God has put it into our hearts. The Lord does not abandon those who have <u>repented</u> of their sins.

THE BLOOD

One night in a church service a young woman felt the tug of God at her heart. She responded to God's call and accepted Jesus as her Lord and Savior. The young woman had a very rough past involving alcohol, drugs, and prostitution. But the change in her was evident. As time went on she became a faithful member of the church. She eventually became involved in the ministry, teaching young children. It was not very long until this faithful young woman had caught the eye and heart of the pastor's son. The relationship grew and they began to make wedding plans. This is when the problems began. You see, about one half of the church did not think that a woman with a past such as hers was suitable for a pastor's son. The church began to argue and fight about the matter; so they decided to have a meeting. As the people made their arguments and tensions increased, the meeting was getting completely out of hand. The young woman became very upset about all the things being brought up about her past. As she began to cry the pastor's son stood to speak. He could not bear the pain it was causing his wife to be. He began to speak and his statement was this: "My fiancée's past is not what is on trial here. What you are questioning is the ability of the blood of Jesus to wash away sin. Today you have put the blood of Jesus on trial. So, does it wash away sin or not?" The whole church began to weep as they realized that they had been slandering the blood

Epilogue

of the Lord Jesus Christ. Too often, even as Christians, we bring up the past and use it as a weapon against our brothers and sisters. Forgiveness is a very foundational part of the Gospel of our Lord Jesus Christ.

This book was written to deal with the <u>perceived</u> threat of danger regarding having sex offenders living in our communities. The facts concerning the numbers that do re-offend show that in reality sex offenders (contrary to popular belief) have the lowest recidivism rate of any other classification of crime. Fewer sex offenders commit new crimes, than do drug dealers, burglars, robbers, or any other type of criminal. None of these have any restrictions as to where they can live when they get out of prison. Is the murderer, drug addict, or alcoholic any less threat to our communities? Yet, after serving their time, sex offenders are treated like lepers.

What can we do? First, we need to reduce the fear level. Then we need to pressure our legislators to stop making more repressive laws, and re-visit the existing laws to reflect on the nature of the crime and not treat all sex offenders like the ones who commit the more serious crimes.

REFERENCES

Chapter One
(1) **http://www.dc.state.ks.us/publications/sex-offender-housing-restrictions**
Kansas Department of Corrections
900 SW Jackson Topeka, KS 66612-1284

Chapter Two
(1) www.focusonthefamily.com
Focus On The Family
Colorado Springs, CO 80995

(2) www.lote.org
Living On The Edge
PO Box 80069
Atlanta, GA 30366

Chapter Three
(1) www.hometimes.org
Home Times Family Newspaper
P.O. Box 22547
West Palm Beach, FL 33416

(2) www.everymanministries.com
New Life Ministries
P.O. Box 1018
Laguna Beach, CA 92652

Chapter Four
(1) www.ncianet.org/publicpolicy/publications/ MoreEffectiveLegis_March2007.pdf
National Center on Institutions and Alternatives, Inc.
7222 Ambassador Road
Baltimore, Maryland 21244

(2) http://www.csom.org/pubs/pubs.html#csombro
Center for Sex Offender Management
c/o Center for Effective Public Policy
8403 Colesville Road, Suite 720
Silver Spring, MD 20910

Chapter Six
(1) http://www.ojp.usdoj.gov/bjs/crimoff.htm#sex
Bureau of Justice Statistics
810 Seventh Street, NW
Washington, DC **20531**

(2) www.stopitnow.com/asit_epidemic.html
Stop It Now
351 Pleasant Street, Suite B-319
Northampton, MA 01060

Chapter Eight
(1)   http://www.americanchronicle.com/articles/viewArticle. asp?articleID=29589
By Niki Delson niki@delko.net

References:

(2) https://www.atsa.com/pdfs/ppResidenceRestrictions.pdf
By Professor Jill S. Levinson
Lynn University
3601 North Military Trail
Boca Raton, Fla. 33431

(3) http://www.ojp.usdoj.gov/bjs/crimoff.htm#sex
Bureau of Justice Statistics
810 Seventh Street, NW
Washington, DC **20531**

Chapter Ten
(1) www.theophostic.com
Theophostic Prayer Ministries
P.O. Box 489
Campbellsville, KY 42719

Chapter Thirteen
(1) http://faculty.ncwc.edu/toconnor/soc/355lect01.htm
http://bahai-library.com/encyclopedia/prejudice.html

Chapter Fourteen
(1) From HeartQuotes: http://www.heartquotes.net/fear.html

WE GET MAIL

Here are just a few of the letters we received:

From a lady in California

Dear Dick,

I want to thank you for your ministries! I wish I could find a ministry like yours in my area. My husband is serving a 12-year sentence in Prison for molesting my daughter. My story is long, but I'd like to share part of it with you. When I first learned the truth I was full of rage and hate! I thought my husband was the lowest form of a human being and didn't deserve my mercy. At the time, due to actions of my husband, we were living in my parent's motor home on some property they were care taking. My husband was working and his job provided us with insurance for the family. I knew once the authorities got involved I'd be blamed and they'd judge us for living in a motor home. So I kept what my husband did to myself and planned to save enough money to get my 2 children into a home before we turned him in. I felt he should at least help us before he was incarcerated. The hate and anger I had toward him was slowly destroying me! I prayed and asked God to please help me, that this was too much for me to do alone. I had just lashed out at him and he was outside as far away from me as he could get. I'm not a violent person, but I lost control and started hitting him. I couldn't even stand to look at him. God said to me that my husband's soul was just as important to him as mine

The Modern Day Leper

and that I was to go to him and tell him that I was sorry for hitting him and that it was the sin I hated not the man. At first I thought no way! That was the last thing I wanted to do. God urged me saying you asked for my help now trust me! I went and found my husband and told him all God told me to say and then I walked away as fast as I could. As I walked away I realized the hate I felt toward my husband starting being replaced with compassion. We started going to church as a family and talked to the pastor about what my husband did. I knew no matter what my husband needed to face the consequences of his actions. I didn't plan on months passing, yet felt it was in God's hands. My father ended up being diagnosed with cancer of the esophagus and all the stress was too much. I sent my daughter to visit her older sister in Northern California, so she could have a break from all the stress. I was trying to find a way to turn my husband in without our family being torn apart. Well, my daughter told her sister and the police arrested my husband at work and flew him up to Northern California where my daughters were. He pled guilty to spare my daughter going through a trial. The police threatened to arrest me and didn't want to hear anything I had to say. Sadly because I talked of forgiveness and rehabilitation for my husband I lost custody of my daughter. Her older sister was given guardianship of her and I was treated like a criminal. It's been a long hard road and after a year and a half I was finally allowed to see and talk to my daughter: No one supports me staying in contact with my husband or staying married to him. Before he was arrested he accepted Christ as his savior and is involved in a prison fellowship. His own parents want nothing to do with him! Since all of this happened I've been searching for help to stay married to him and get him therapy. Sadly I know my older daughter will stop letting me see my grandchildren if she finds out I'm helping him. I tell myself that it is in God's hands and that I'm doing what God has asked of me and that is more important. Any suggestions on how I can get my daughter to be more open to me helping my husband? She sees it as me being weak, yet it has taken a lot of strength for me to get this far.

God Bless you and all you are doing!

From a man applying for a position with our ministry
Up until May 2005 I had a wonderful life. Wife, kids, career, and then I was accused of touching one of my daughters friends on the butt by her father, who was in the midst of a nasty divorce and custody battle with the mother. The poorly qualified and conviction motivated military, court martialed me in May 2006. I was found not guilty, but an agenda motivated and very hostile military judge kept sending the panel back until she got what she wanted. I am innocent and forced to register as a SO until my appeal gets seen and then conviction set aside.

I have a wife and three daughters along with a home in Illinois. I live in Florida (by choice), sparing my family this stigma until the appeal process hopefully rights this wrong. I have found myself to be 'unemployable' and unable to support myself much less my family. I have many skills to offer in administration and hope to be considered for a position or at least given guidance.

From a lady in Georgia
I belong to the quintessential American Christian family. I am a 50-year-old white female living in a rural area of America with my husband complete with a vegetable garden, chickens, and everything else that you would equate with a rural lifestyle. I have two sons, one is an executive at a respected corporation and the other is an honor student at the university he attends. My husband is a very loving Christian man that knows more about the Bible than anyone I know. In obedience to the scriptures we try to "remember the prisoners" (Heb. 13:3) and we have established a small, yet effective prison ministry. But, I have a deep dark secret. I am among a group of the most persecuted people in America. Why, you ask? **My husband is a registered sex offender.**

The sex offender registry is the greatest violations of human and civil rights in America today, but no one is willing to touch it. No one wants to appear to be against "protecting the children." The press, politicians, and some church leaders try to convince us that every sex offender is an irredeemable monster. If they are not watched, they will hide behind a tree at your child's school, indiscriminately grab children, carry them off, and do horrible things to them. Meet my husband, the horrible monster.

ABANDONED AND ABUSED

My husband was abandoned at birth. At three weeks old he was adopted by a couple. His adopted father was a World War II hero and a law enforcement official. His father was a spy during the war and was captured behind enemy lines. During his stay in a prison camp, he was physically tortured in such a way he could not have children. No one ever talked about the trauma of war back in the mid-1950's, but my husband's father was obviously traumatized. This was a trait he passed on to his children. My husband was physically beaten, tortured, and emotionally traumatized by his father when he was growing up. Many people in the community knew what was happening, but no one said anything because his father was a war hero and a respected member of the community. My husband and I grew up together and dated in high school, but as a lot of high school romances go we broke up and went our separate ways. My husband left home and married a woman that was equally as abusive to him as his father. The abuse was more sexual than physical. How does a woman sexually abuse a man? She does it by being frigid and using sex as an instrument of control. They were married for nineteen years. My husband was finally fed up with the abuse and left her. He was now angry, confused, and not sure where his life was headed. He moved to a different town and got a job working for a computer company as a technician. He met a woman there and started dating her. This woman had been investigated for the poisoning death of her former husband. She was not only abusive, but scary. She applied and was accepted for a program that sent her to Antarctica for six months. They take lay people to Antarctica for six months during the summer to help scientists. She abandoned her nine-year old daughter and a son to go there. During her absence, my husband thought the relationship was over and remarried. When she returned she became very angry and she said, "If I can't have him, no one can." She filed charges against him for molesting her daughter. There was no evidence against him or any witnesses that saw him do anything to the child, only hearsay and statements coerced from the daughter by therapists and psychologists. When accused of molesting a child in some states, the law states that there doesn't need to be any witnesses or evidence. My husband felt backed into a corner and pleaded no contest to lesser charges. He was sentenced to four years in prison.

THE HEALING BEGINS

Alone again, because his second wife had divorced him during this time, he walked in prison thinking he was dead as a convicted child molester. But, the Lord had other plans. It was then the Lord put his hand on my husband's life and began working miracles of healing and protection in his life. My husband was put in a cell with a man that had a very violent past and was in prison for a violent crime. They lived in peace for awhile, but one afternoon my husband returned to his cell and the man punched him in the face dislocating his jaw. My husband didn't fight back, he only pinned the man up against the bed to stop him. When the guards finally broke up the fight, both were sent to "the hole" and the guards investigated the fight. The guards were completely astonished when the other guy assumed total responsibility for the fight. (This never happens in prison) Because my husband's cellmate was the leader of a gang, my husband was no longer safe in general population. He was transferred to another prison. My husband had been trying to get into therapy and thought this was his chance. He was very upset when the bus turned and went to wrong direction. The Lord knew what he was doing, because the prison my husband was sent to had many strong Christian brother's incarcerated there. This was where his healing began. They ministered to him by praying with him, teaching him the true meaning of Christian love, and teaching him the word. It was a truly amazing time in his life. The healing process had already begun in my husband's life and the Lord was going to finish it. He often felt the Lord touching his heart and healing him in his prison cell. But, the only way to prove my husband was serious about changing was to receive secular therapy. The healing that started there followed him to different facilities where he received therapy.

SECULAR THERAPY

Secular therapy, especially for sex offenders, isn't about healing but about proving the psychiatric communities long held position that sex offenders can't be healed. Therapists, who work with sex offenders, brainwash them into believing they are always dangerous, will always need therapy, and can never be healed. About half way through the therapy, my husband faced his first polygraph. Before the test they made him fill out a 175-page report of every sexual encounter he had ever had in his entire life. About a week before the test they fired him from his work assignment and changed his cellmate. They put my husband in with a Jewish man thinking the two would not get along. They forced these two emotionally disturbing life changes on my husband in a deliberate effort to affect his polygraph test since a disturbed emotional state causes physically irregularities that are interpreted as being deceptive. After the test, my husband was called into his therapist's office. She seemed visibly upset. When my husband asked her what was wrong she replied, "Your polygraph came back non-deceptive. We wanted to charge you with another felony for molesting your daughters." My husband was also informed he was the only person in the nine year history of the program to pass the polygraph on the first try. As the therapy progressed, my husband again found himself with a different cellmate. The man was in with a life sentence for murder. My husband was again called into his therapist's office. He was informed that the man had planned to kill him while he slept, but something had stopped the man and he confessed to prison authorities.

ON PAROLE

After being released from therapy it was time for my husband to go before the parole board. He was granted release as one of the only sex offenders to ever be released on parole. His mother had promised he could come home to her house after his release from prison, but when she saw he had to register with hometown police, she refused. She didn't want to be embarrassed because some of the law enforcement officials still remembered my husband's father. His new parole plan put him back in the same small town where his "crime" was committed. This was an almost sure setup for failure, but the Lord again would not allow this to happen. My husband, who was not even dangerous enough to arrest before his prison sentence (being summoned to court only by a subpoena), was now the considered most dangerous person in the community. He was released as "highly likely to re-offend." His parole plan required him to have a parole officer, a therapist, made him wear a GPS tracking device, made him do urinalysis (even though he had never done drugs), and he had to register. The halfway house he was assigned to would not let him in, but he was able to secure better living arrangements in a mobile home park with the help of his sister. He was required to get a job. It took him awhile, but he finally found two jobs; one at a meat packing plant and the other at a restaurant. His therapist also wanted to put him back in prison for a minor infraction. One of his supposed "victims" was his younger sister. While on parole, his sister was one of his greatest supporters. She had helped him find a place to live and was one of his support people. She was an ex-drug addict and prostitute that had cleaned up her life and pursued a career as a social worker. Because of her background, she had worked with my husband's parole officer. They would call her in when they suspected a parolee was playing them. She could tell immediately if they were. The therapist believed that it was a violation of my husband's parole to have contact with a previous victim. She also believed that he was grooming his sister to molest here again. The therapist called my husband into her office. She was upset because she couldn't find a tape recorder. She began to grill my husband on his relationship with his sister. He told her all the information she asked, but stated emphatically that he was not grooming or molesting his sister. He was then called to a meeting with his parole officer. He was told that the therapist had wanted to file charges against him for molesting his sister, but couldn't because she couldn't find a tape recorder so there was no proof of their conversation. The parole officer had also talked with my husband's sister. After the conversation the parole officer stated, "I talked with your sister. I believer the charges your therapist tried to bring against you are bullshit." It was after that; my husband found out he was being watched by police twenty-four hours a day. While the police department was watching him to protect the children in the area, they observed the mobile home next door was very active. An investigation revealed it had a meth-lab and there were two young boys living at the residence.

FULFILLMENT OF GODS VISIONS

Four months later, my husband was now off parole, and was able to start fulfilling some of the God given visions he had had while in prison. He had told some of his Christian brothers in prison about these visions, but they dismissed them saying they would never come true. His plan was to work at the meat packing plant for a year, save his money, and move to where I lived. But, he was threatened at work by a couple of employees. They said they knew about his crime and would kill him if he returned. We both felt this was a clear signal from God that he should move. He did.

Vision Number one, marrying me
As previously stated, we had dated in high school. I was a bright spot in his abusive upbringing and he had never forgotten me. We had re-united right before he went into prison and had become great friends, but I DID NOT want to get married. I had the Lord and that was enough. We were a good team. Why mess it up with someone else? Then the Lord changed my mind. One month, one week, and one day after he arrived, we were married.

Vision number two, playing guitar and entertaining for money
When my husband was adopted, his adoptive parents stated that they wanted a child that had entertainers in his family background. My husband is an entertainer. It is in his blood. If he can't entertain anyone he will entertain himself. However, his adoptive family didn't know what to do with the entertainer they had. They bought him a guitar, but then ridiculed him for playing it. They further discouraged him from being an entertainer by telling him he would become a drug addict if he went into the entertainment industry. This stopped him for awhile, but he had it in his blood. It was his dream when he was released from prison to play guitar

and sing for a living. My father was ill at the time and was paying me to take care of him so I ample time to go with my husband and show him places that had entertainment. It took only a few months to get enough gigs to bring in good money.

Vision number three, meeting the leader of a prison ministry

There was a man that had a prison ministry and sent my husband a Bible study and a Bible while he was in prison. This had been a huge influence on my husband's life. Much to our surprise, the man lived less than five miles from us. We were able to connect with him and have established a great friendship.

Vision number four, living in the country

My husband's adoptive parents had purchased a ranch when he was twelve years old. They told him that if he worked really hard when they retired he could have the ranch. This was not to happen, because when they retired they sold the ranch for the money. His dream was always to live on a ranch in the country again. But, I was resistant to this idea. I was raised on a ranch and hated every minute of it. When I left home I moved to the city, vowing never to live in the country again. I was a city dweller for over thirty years and I loved every minute of it. After my dad died, I was left with some money. He had bought property that he had never seen in a different state. We decided to go look at the property my father had left. We were contemplating a move because the condo we lived in was becoming very cramped, but we weren't sure exactly what we were going to do. The property my father had purchased was not acceptable, but we found a beautiful fifty acres with a house, barn, mountain view, and established business. I fell in love with it. We were able to pay cash for the property. We went home, put the condo up for sale, and had a cash offer in four days.

Vision number five, having a prison ministry
After prison, it was my husband's dream was to establish his own prison ministry. We have been able to establish one with the help of our friend. We have pen pals, my husband writes Bible studies that we send into the prisons, and we have financially helped prisoner's families. We have the possibility of receiving a grant to establish an aftercare on our property. The miracles keep coming faster and getting bigger, but I am sure there are still visions the Lord have given us that are as of yet unfulfilled.

As the wife of a registered sex offender, what am I supposed to do?
What am I supposed to do? Should I believe what society that is made up of fallible, corruptible humans believes about sex offenders? Or should I believe what an infallible, incorruptible God says? The church has all but abandoned us. We have been told about discriminatory policies that prohibit sex offenders from attending church. We also hear of background checks being done by churches all the time. The only check that should be necessary in the Body of Christ is a check of the anointing of God in the person's life. We have been asked at least four times to leave churches when

they find out about my husband's past. Is this Christian? Is church only for the "healthy"? What happened to the churches Biblical mandate to be an instrument of hope and healing? Have churches become afraid of having sinners in their midst or afraid of being sued? Remember the next time you feel it necessary to move into one of those "sex offender free" neighborhoods, you may have to live next door to a sex offender in heaven. As members of the body of Christ we must remember we are all sinners saved by grace.

ABOUT THE AUTHOR

The year was 1966. Finding out that his wife had cancer, Dick began to seek a higher purpose in life other than his work as a private detective. This also led to his overcoming addictions to alcohol and sexual perversions. Following the death of his wife in 1980 he attended the Gospel Crusade Institute of Ministry in Bradenton, Florida. After his graduation he served as chaplain of the newly formed "Gospel Rescue Mission of the Palm Beaches" in West Palm Beach, Florida, and soon became executive director of that mission. In 1983 Dick married Margaret Howe, who had been widowed a year earlier. Together they started the Regeneration Center a ministry to alcoholics and drug addicts. They continued to serve at this in-residency recovery center, until they resigned in 1990 to form Matthew 25 Ministries, a prison ministry whose main focus is prison after care. They acquired their first house in 1991. Over the years they were faithful in small things while waiting for the Lord to fulfill the larger vision He had given Dick. With the large number of prisoners being released into our communities, Dick's vision was to be able to assist more ex-offenders. He then received a burden to assist the modern day lepers; those charged with sexual crimes. In May of 2000 their ministry received a donation of 21 acres of land with existing facilities in a rural area in Okeechobee County, Florida and The P.A.C.T. Center (Prison After Care Treatment) was formed. They started this phase of the ministry with 10-student beds and operated this men's facility for 30 months until a zoning issue forced it to close in January 2003. In 2005 they sold the ranch property and acquired another home in Okeechobee County. They re-established their aftercare program for sex-offenders, which as of this writing is still in operation.

Made in the USA